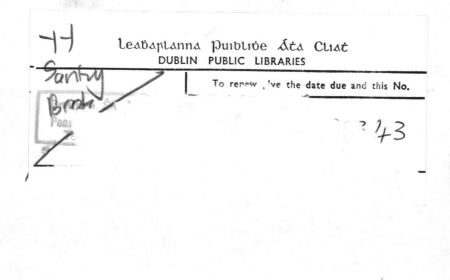

The Incomparable Game

Also by Colin Cowdrey

CRICKET TODAY
TIME FOR REFLECTION
TACKLE CRICKET THIS WAY

The Incomparable Game

by

COLIN COWDREY

HODDER AND STOUGHTON

LONDON SYDNEY AUCKLAND TORONTO

Contents

Illustrations

ACKNOWLEDGEMENTS

All photographs, except where
indicated, are reproduced by
permission of Central Press
Photos Ltd.

Foreword

As I lay in my hospital bed after the operation on my broken Achilles tendon, I was very conscious of people's reaction as they visited or telephoned. I could sense that as they tried hard to bring good cheer they thought that I would not come back into the game. The injury was repairable, but at the age of thirty-seven they realised how hard it could be to raise an appetite again for the hurly burly of the sporting arena.

"Was it really 1950 when you started — aren't you bored with it now?" I am surprised how often I have been challenged on this point recently and usually this is followed by an expression of astonishment how one could continue to raise a schoolboy zest for this extraordinary game of ours.

But that is just it. The game of cricket keeps tugging me in the way that fascinated so many over the years. For me it has been an education. It has taken me to most parts of the British Isles and, through cricket, I have come to love and know my country and its folk more than I would otherwise have done.

Furthermore, cricket has taken me across the world. Ashamedly, I play at Dover and Folkestone every year, but have never crossed the twenty miles of water to France. Yet I feel that I know Australia, New Zealand and the West Indies as if they were my home. I have been lucky enough to tour South Africa, India, Pakistan and Ceylon. Except the South Pole I have played cricket wherever the Union Jack has flown. I have known the fickleness of the publicity medium, yet appreciated the true warmth and loyalty of the solid core of cricket lovers. I have known the agony of hitting rock bottom yet I have been lucky enough to touch the heights often enough to keep me striving.

One way and another for me it has been — and always will be — the incomparable game.

Schoolboy Cricketer

In 1938 I was being brought back from India as a five-year old, having just won the ship's fancy dress prize in a scaled-down version of Henry Cotton's golfing ensemble, when my father rushed into the cabin, tore me from the bunk and carried me up on deck. The whole movement was executed at top speed, much faster than he had moved in any of the boat drills that were part of the voyage.

On deck he pointed to a lighted ship that was rapidly over-hauling us and informed me with some excitement that it was carrying the Australian cricket team to England. Then, after a pause, he added solemnly: "On that ship is Don Bradman." Clearly the Australians excited him, but Bradman was God, or that was the impression he gave me.

So at the age of five I was given my first intimation that Sir Donald was a man apart. The notion has been confirmed many times since.

We spent the summer of 1938 together as a family in England. The memories are jumbled. My father went to the Oval Test match and saw Leonard Hutton score his 364. I was left behind to

15

listen to it on the radio and even now I can recall the chocolate texture of the voice of Howard Marshall, the commentator. Apart from Hutton's, Hammond's and Fingleton's were the names that predominated. I wonder what was said to make them stick for more than thirty years?

My parents went back to India and I was left in an England at war that had no first-class cricket until around 1942. Duly I paid my first visit to Lord's, an awe-struck member of a prep. school party under the command of a master. Wally Hammond made a hundred which means that of all the millions who have watched cricket through the years nobody can have had a better introduction to it than I had.

I recall more names from that period...Learie Constantine, Keith Miller and Denis Compton.

I mention this gradual gathering of names in my mind because it marks an essential difference in the watching habits of the young people of my day and those now. There was no television to make the faces and personalities of the cricketers as familiar as those of the persons around the breakfast table. To us, cricketers were distant names and performances. We knew who they were and what they had done, but except from cigarette cards we had little idea what they looked like. We worshipped just as hard as they do now, but in a more abstract way.

What sort of game was cricket in my early boyhood when it was played by men who had learned it on the true pitches of the 1930s under an lbw law kinder to batsmen than anything since?

It was essentially, I think, an amateur game and an attacking one. From what I have gathered over the years I doubt if defence started to become a significant factor until the last two or three years before the war. Jack Hobbs was the master batsman prior to 1930 and I imagine him to be a great attacking batsman. Obviously he must have possessed defensive strokes, but they were to get him out of trouble. By nature he must have been a committed attacking player.

I have heard people say that when Surrey won the toss at the Oval in good conditions, Hobbs' target was always a hundred before lunch. Many was the time apparently, when he was around eighty or ninety when the break came. My evidence for saying this comes from people who played with him, like Percy Chapman, and others who followed his cricket with fanaticism, like my father.

I first walked to the wicket for Kent as a schoolboy in 1950, and I am going to look at some of the people and outstanding events in the two decades of cricket since then. The players who dominated my early years in the game were players who had played in the '40s — such as wartime activity would permit — and who mostly learned their cricket in the '30s.

The drama and the uncertainty of the South African tour of England is behind us and we can now move into the '70s with a spring in our step. M.C.C.'s tour of Australia is the first matter on the agenda, and to me, this series is the ultimate in a cricketer's life and ambition. We have seen so many changes in recent years, changes both at the heart of the technique of our game and just as many in the presentation of our game to a more selective public. As you will find, I am an optimist for the game and I see the '70s as something to look forward to, but before I delve into the future, will you join me as I sketch in the background.

My father would dash to the Oval during his lunch-break, watch Hobbs score twenty or thirty runs and then make for the

17

Tube and return to his office happier than most men in London. Percy Fender, the Surrey captain of the period, is another who had talked to me of Hobbs' dedication to attack.

In my own county, Kent, Frank Woolley serves as an example. He watches me bat and almost gives up in despair. He does not appear to understand why we defend at all, and I doubt if he was ever really restricted to defence. Most of his hundreds seem to have come in two and a quarter to two and a half hours.

Leslie Ames, now the manager of Kent, scored a hundred hundreds and never took more than three hours over one except in a Test Match. Ames claims that he never played the forward defensive stroke. His method was to play back. If he went forward he let the bat go through in a drive.

The freedom went out of batting with the alteration in the lbw law in 1935, a piece of legislation that brought the seam bowler into prominence, killed off the wrist-spinner and made survival so often the limit of a batsman's ambition. Almost every legislative move that has been made since the war — and there have been dozens — has been aimed at undoing the harm inflicted in 1935.

Under the old lbw law, life for the batsman was straightforward and challenging. With the ball having to pitch between wicket and wicket to have him lbw he was free of the restrictions which have been imposed on batsmen ever since by bowlers bringing the ball in from outside the off-stump. As a result all the back-foot strokes were open to him. He could cut or play past extra-cover or hit back past the bowler as Hammond did, or wide of mid-on in the way Peter May did in recent years. Only his inability to play the strokes restricted him. With it all, he was still in a position to leap forward and attack if the fancy took him. So there was really no

18

SIR DONALD BRADMAN IN COMMAND Leslie Ames (left) and Godfrey Evans (right) have one thing in common, apart from being fine England wicket-keepers. They have both spent hours waiting in vain behind the Australian Master. His two favourite shots are shown here, the cut and the hook. Wherever the captain placed third man, he seemed to have the knack of placing the ball either side. Similarly, he could place the pull and the hook with disarming precision.

JARDINE AND LARWOOD. It was Bradman's prodigious run scoring which brought out the ruthless streak in Jardine, the deployment of Harold Larwood to a plan and the birth of Body-Line. Here you see Jardine's poker face, which always seemed to be crowned with a Harlequin cap. Across the cricket grounds of Australia this stood for a fearsome strength which even they found difficult to accept.

reason to play defensively.

And because the batsmen attacked the bowlers did as well, probably in the belief that in this welter of stroke play their best chance of success lay in bowling straight and waiting for the error. Moreover, with most batsmen thinking in terms of back-foot play, the bowlers sought to pitch the ball up.

The game then must have been like a head-on collision of cavalry. Maurice Tate first brought it home to me how aggressive was the bowling. He was the coach during the two years I was captain at Tonbridge and it was to him I would go when I needed advice.

It was Maurice who made me aware that captaincy was an art in itself and in my determination to succeed I would spend the two history periods before play began on a Saturday morning writing out the field placings for my bowlers right down to the detail of having players named for the various positions.

Coming back in the coach from a match in which our bowlers had been so heavily punished that I had counted the fieldsmen to see if I had lost a couple, I asked Maurice for tips about placing a containing field. He was non-committal to the point of being unhelpful.

I persisted until in the end I decided that the only way to get what I wanted was to question him on an actual case. I recalled the Test Match at Leeds in 1930 when Tate was bowling and Bradman scored a hundred in each session of the day. What was the position at tea? I wanted to know.

Bradman was around 200, he said, and the new ball had just been taken. He thought they had had an over at each end with it, a popular tactic then because it gave them two bites at the new ball, before and after the break.

Right, I said. The score was astronomical, the pitch good, the outfield fast — what was your aim once he got in after tea?

"To bowl him out," said Maurice. "I aimed at the off-stump and pitched the ball up. If he missed I would have bowled him."

But he didn't miss. He scored 334 runs before Tate got him.

When he got down to explanations, Tate, one of the great bowlers of the pre-war period, said that basically his field was always the same. He had three slips, a gully, third-man, cover-point and mid-off. If the punishment became extreme he would shift the third-slip to extra-cover. That was the only concession of any size he made to defence.

In the case of Bradman he delivered every ball to dismiss him. He neither bowled wide of the off-stump nor tried to restrain him by aiming at the leg-stump — the latter policy was used by Alec Bedser, a similar bowler to Tate, in 1948. I would think that Bedser was the last bowler of that type to insist on keeping a mid-off and a mid-on, so as to be able to keep pitching the ball to a full length.

The Tate philosophy of attack at all times seems to have been shared by most of the bowlers of that period. I have never heard it suggested that Larwood, with the notable exception of the 1932 tour of Australia, ever bowled anything but straight. Except in later years when he cannily decided to push the ball through when the punishment became unbearable, Tich Freeman bowled only for dismissals. And in an age when leg-spinning was still a worth-while vogue, one cannot imagine Walter Robins, Ian Peebles or Greville Stevens being anything except belligerent. Douglas Wright never bowled defensively.

To me, a modern captain, the whole game of those days has an attractive but rather incredulous air about it. I listen to old players talk with much the same kind of suspended belief that children save for listening to fairy tales. I wonder if anybody can remember the exact date when the term "Bowling tight" was first used?

In 1935, the legislators, satiated with runs, changed the lbw law so that a batsman could be dismissed lbw by the ball cutting back from outside the off-stump providing his pads were between wicket and wicket at the moment of contact. It was a classic case of over-kill.

In essence I think you can say that the confusion and despair that has plagued the game ever since was caused unwittingly by Don Bradman's skill. He was too good, too successful as a batsman, with the result that he caused developments in the game that would have been beyond the power of the ordinary player.

* * *

From the time he started Sir Donald Bradman was a man of influence in the game. He played his first Test Match against England in 1928. In 1930, he took England by storm. By 1932 "bodyline" had been invented just to take care of him. Douglas Jardine, I would think, was the first English captain to go into a series with a comprehensive plan aimed at the stopping of one player.

Whatever may be said about "bodyline" — and little can be found in its favour — it marked the first stage in the now accepted analytical approach to cricket. For the first time selected bowlers working to pre-arranged fields were aimed at the stopping of opposing batsmen. Later we were to see O'Reilly stifling the powers of Wally Hammond with a leg-stump attack. There were other targets in the Australian team for Larwood and company of course, but Bradman was the main one. He was the reason behind this plan.

In the context of the gifted but casual amateur captain who was the accepted figure of the time, it was a revolutionary one. I have heard nothing in talks with county captains of the period — among them Percy Fender, freely named as the best captain never to lead England — to make me think that their tactical planning was in the same category as that of Jardine, Bradman himself later on, Hutton or the modern captains. They had their tricks but they appear to have been confined to the occasional full toss, the trap at long-on, etc. and various psychological ploys. Jardine brought a different concept to captaincy.

Between 1930 and 1948 the fashion in leadership changed until there came the ultimate in tough, efficient, premeditated leadership. Predictably it was Bradman who embodied it. He came to England for his last tour, led his side through five months of cricket unbeaten and by his ruthless approach — no less ruthless than Jardine's — professionalised the thinking. I think particularly of his use of fast bowlers.

Everything he did in his position as captain of Australia was canny and well thought-out. He arrived in England with a battery of fast bowlers at a time when our administrators in a moment of incomprehension had agreed to the new ball being taken every fifty-five overs. It was an open invitation to batter us with fast bowling for the twenty-five days of the series. This he proceeded to do with the utmost dedication.

Ray Lindwall bowled 222 overs. Keith Miller, who was also

one of the side's main batsmen, bowled 138. Bill Johnston, a left-hander who came on after these two, got through 309. There were two other main bowlers, neither of whom was quick but only one of whom was slow. The more important of them was Ernie Toshack.

Toshack was a slow-medium left-hander who bowled defensively at the leg-stump and gave Lindwall, Miller and Johnston the few overs rest they needed before they took yet another new ball and launched themselves again. His contribution was 173 overs. Ian Johnson, a flighty off-spinner, was the only genuine slow bowler to get recognition and he bowled 183 overs. He was probably in the side through being a reasonable batsman, a good slip fielder and because there was a theory that he troubled Len Hutton.

The Australians that year played power cricket. Because of their success they were constantly compared with Warwick Armstrong's side of 1921 in the interminable argument about which was the best team ever to represent Australia. I should be surprised if there were much doubt about it. Gregory and Macdonald swept aside England in '21, yet there was never much suggestion that theirs was an organised slaying. English cricket was desperately weak at the time and in Gregory and Macdonald Armstrong had two fast bowlers who needed no more than an invitation to bowl to win the match for him.

It was said that English cricket was also weak in 1948 and so it was. But then it was the bowling that was below standard. Washbrook, Hutton, Edrich and Compton formed the front line of batting, and I can only say that I have played in many England sides where those four would have been welcome.

23

Bradman planned their destruction and it was in this question of leadership that there probably existed the greatest difference between the Australian sides of 1921 and 1948. Sir Donald won the matches brutally and decisively by using the circumstances as he found them. He did what he felt he had to do as Australia's captain, and there can be no criticism of him on this score.

Yet if anything, his methods were too successful, for they proved unarguably the case for relying on the quick bowlers and ignoring the spinners. The deadening effect on the game of fast bowlers walking back, the constant manipulating of the new ball rule in an effort to deduce their importance — these have been the side effects of Bradman's 1948 triumph.

As an enlightened administrator who cares deeply for the game and its future, I wonder sometimes how he feels now about the methods of 1948. Ultimately I suppose, you come back to the question: Is the captain's job to do more than win?

As a moulder of fashions of captaincy, Bradman's contribution was significant. As a batsman his influence on the game was devastating.

I feel certain it was largely as a result of his success on the marled wickets of the 1930's that the lbw law was changed. Much was made of the ugliness of Herbert Sutcliffe's method of padplay and clearly there was a desire to counter this development. But there was an even bigger desire to do something about Bradman's unfailing ability to make huge scores and indeed the large number of dull drawn matches. It was felt that the pendulum had swung too far for the batsmen and it was now time to favour the bowlers.

So started the trouble of our time. I cannot imagine that anyone foresaw in-slant bowling. Few foresaw Len Hutton's forward push which was to become the key stroke in a changing game of reduced aggression. In a relatively short time there developed a generation of batsmen, myself among them, for whom the back foot was of minor importance. It is revealing that it was not until in casual conversation ten years ago that I came to realise how wide was the range of back-foot strokes which we were not able to use much. That is a measure of how obsessional and necessary the front foot has become to us.

Most cricketers I am convinced, do not realise that there is a greater variety of strokes off the back foot than the front. The very movement on to the front foot seems to suggest aggression. Yet there is no doubt that all the great stroke players have been predominantly back-foot players who have moved forward into their stroke only when they have seen that the ball has been pitched up. Now there is a change back in the lbw law and it may take two or three seasons before we can judge whether it can influence the game for the better. I believe it will.

* * *

The period 1946-50 saw a famine in fast bowlers in English cricket. There was not one genuine fast bowler in English cricket, except Warwickshire's Tom Pritchard and he was a New Zealander.

England, seven years without cricket, went to Australia in 1946 and were beaten by the speed of Lindwall and Miller, two men who were to become the best fast bowlers of their time. There was neither surprise nor shame in that defeat.

Batsmen through the County Championship, piled up runs as they have not been piled up since. Compton made 1947 his own year while the pitches have become legendary for their perfection. Yet how good were they in reality, without a fast bowler in the country to test them? County batsmen would raise their eyebrows at the thought of playing Tom Pritchard in the next match apparently, yet he was not genuinely fast like Tyson, Statham, Trueman, Loader, the bowlers of the 1950's.

In 1947-48 Weekes, Worrell and Walcott took England apart in the West Indies. In 1948 Bedser's opening bowling partners against Australia were Edrich, Coxon, Pollard, and in the last Test, Alan Watkins, a medium-paced all-rounder from Glamorgan. Without fast bowlers, every match must have seemed a bit lopsided.

Yet the change was close. By 1949 Bedser had become a great bowler; Jackson and Gladwin of Derbyshire were a force; Trueman eighteen years old, played his first game for Yorkshire; a year later Loader appeared for Surrey; and in the winter of 1950 Statham was flown to Australia to reinforce the M.C.C. party.

There were other developments in types of bowling as well. Laker had gone to West Indies, and whilst showing promise, he was given rather a hiding. The 1948 Australians had added to his suffering and he disappeared for a time but by 1950, when he ruined a Test trial by taking eight wickets for two runs, there were indications of the fame to come.

Bob Appleyard, for two or three years the best bowler I ever saw, was preparing to take 200 wickets in the 1950 season. Lock and Wardle were coming along and Trevor Bailey was in the throes of changing from an ordinary tearaway fast bowler into a fine medium pacer.

Even in this time of strife, the nucleus of the strong England attack of the 1950's was shaping itself.

* * *

Some time from the late '40s onward, there took place the most meaningful technical change of my time in cricket. The bowlers changed the length.

Before 1935 when ninety per cent of the batsmen spent ninety per cent of the time playing strokes off the back foot, the bowlers naturally pitched a full length. It had obvious virtues plus the less obvious one that it gave the ball more time to swing.

Afterwards Len Hutton revolutionised the technique of English batting by basing his play on the forward defensive push. It became the accepted method for the majority of English batsmen and by 1950 only the remnants of the back-foot school — Compton and Washbrook for two — were left. The effect on the game was dramatic. In defence, bowlers began to pitch the ball shorter. With batsmen coming forward almost before the ball was bowled there was no longer the same reward in pitching a consistent full length. So there disappeared from bowling the qualities which had made it aggressive. The slow bowlers began to dig the ball in instead of flighting it. The quick bowlers thought less in terms of swing and started to bang the ball into the wicket. Seam bowling as an art was born.

Today there is hardly a bowler in English cricket who does not bruise the ball on the pitch; the genuine swing bowlers are few and far between.

* * *

In some ways the lack of bowling of the post-war period had a beneficial effect on the game. It made for batsmen's cricket, and the crowds, swollen to false proportions after the starvation of the war, were entertained more lavishly probably than at any other time in the game's history. Even to this day people who watched cricket at that time talk about the strokes and the runs they saw. To the majority it did not matter that the bowling was below par.

Denis Compton's exploits have earned him a legendary reputation, and indeed he possessed genius. Clearly, he would always have been a great player yet it is unlikely that he would have built the same type of reputation had he started his cricket in 1950. It is an opinion shared by Compton himself.

We both played in the Oval Test Match against Australia in 1956. For Compton it was a comeback after a knee operation and consequently he was some way below his best even though he did score ninety-four. That evening I asked him to ignore the handicap of his knee if he could and to tell me how he felt about batting as it had then become. He expressed a distaste for it. The game had become harder, more restrictive and less enjoyable.

I interpreted that as meaning, among other things, that it had become more organised. At times the pressure becomes unbearable as Ken Barrington found to his cost. Yet in 1947, Compton's golden year, the County game was still being run by amateur captains, amiable in the main and dedicated to the enjoyment of cricket if somewhat limited in their tactical approach. There were exceptions of course, like Brian Sellers of Yorkshire or Walter Robins of Middlesex. Significantly Yorkshire seemed to monopolise the championship title in those days, with Middlesex challenging hard.

* * *

As fast as any Englishman in that period of no fast bowlers, was I suppose, Bill Edrich. Sitting at Lord's watching him on the occasion of Bradman's last innings on the ground, I was filled with that sense of awe that comes to every schoolboy when he sees a bowler he considers fast enough to be fearsome. Edrich, aggressive, fit, terribly busy in his run up, made me think then that it would be impossible for me to play in his class of cricket. He would have been too fast for me and I would never have seen the ball. He frightened me to death just to watch him run up.

This respect was transferred fairly quickly once Bradman got to the wicket and began to compile what everyone said was a typical hundred. The sight of him that sticks in my memory is of his counter to an Edrich bouncer. I don't know whether he picked up a message from the bowler's run up, but he took two little skipping steps away from the stumps and with a horizontal bat lathered the ball down the wicket so that it pitched almost at Edrich's feet on his follow through and caused him to shuffle out of the way like a dancer. Then the ball took off past the umpire like a Bobby Locke low wedge shot and bounced back off the sightscreen at the Nursery End.

That stroke has remained in my memory like a photograph. It tells me everything I want to know about Bradman. I know that when they say he murdered even the best fast bowlers with his hook that it was true. I know also that it must be true when they claim that he was the greatest hooker the game has known. Yet the innings itself I can only recall as clinical and inevitable. He was the efficiency expert par excellence without a flourish or a gesture to his name.

29

There is a story of Bradman's hooking which is now listed in the history of Kent as another example of man's inhumanity to man. The victim was Fred Ridgway, the county's fast bowler who had never seen the Don bat.

So at Canterbury in 1948, as Bradman walked out to take guard, Godfrey Evans and Les Ames, two men whose combined knowledge of Bradman went back nearly twenty years, decided to give him some tactical advice.

"He's got a reputation as a hooker," said Evans, "but when you get to forty it's a different business." Turning to Ames he said: "You used to hook a bit, Les, didn't you, but you had to give it away."

Ames nodded agreement.

"Give him a couple of good length ones around the off-stump," advised Evans, "and then give him the bouncer third ball. You'll get him caught at short-leg."

Ridgway gave the third ball everything. So did Bradman. It pitched among the hydrangeas in front of the Mayor's enclosure scattering the official party, skimmed past two waiters and bounced off the back wall of the tent.

My own cricket started in 1946 as a thirteen-year old. Until then I had been twice to Lord's as a spectator On my third visit I played for Tonbridge against Clifton and was successful enough and attracted sufficient attention to be more of a marked man than a youngster of that age ought to be.

In the holidays I had been attending the cricket school in South London run by Alf Gover and Andy Sandham, and they had sent a note to Ewart Astill, the old Leicestershire and England player who had just been appointed coach to Tonbridge, saying "we suggest you get this boy Cowdrey into your nets as soon as possible. He might make your school team". Three weeks later I was in the side.

During the summer holidays I would go to a farm in Leicestershire and by coincidence Astill was living in Leicester. He got me playing in a few school matches and one week-end picked me for the County side to play in a benefit match for Les Berry. There has been no happier cricket experience in my life than to play in that match — a wide-eyed schoolboy among ten County players. Les Berry batted four, I batted five and we were chasing 150. At the end I was nineteen not out having been dropped three times on purpose, the first time when gully cleverly let the ball slip through his fingers when I had scored one. It was a delicious day.

Kent were playing at Leicester that week-end and I was taken to the dressing room to meet some of the players among whom were Leslie Ames and Brian Valentine, the captain. There was no question at that time of my playing for Kent, for my allegiances were to Surrey (I had been at prep. school at Sutton) or Leicestershire, my annual summer holiday home. In fact, I went to the Oval in September to play for the Surrey Young Amateurs, an expedition which quickly killed Surrey's interest in me.

I specialised in bowling leg-breaks in those days, turning the ball prodigious distances. But not on that magnificent Oval wicket and I was struck harder and for greater distances than anybody who had ever bowled on the ground. Surrey the following year, 1948, did not even look in my direction, and I could not blame them.

At Tonbridge my cricket master was C.H. Knott who used to play for Kent. He suggested to the county that they had better have a look at me in their Young Amateurs' side. In six days I scored 185 against a Sussex side that included Jim Parks, eighty-five against Middlesex and eighty at the Oval. The next year I played for the second eleven; in 1950 for the County team.

* * *

By upbringing and inclination I was a stroke-maker. I had been taught batting on the strict understanding that I was allowed to play myself in for the first fifteen minutes and then I had to hit the ball. Five runs an over was the target. I think maybe the County game then was played to much the same kind of formula. It was still basically an attacking game.

When I look back at my career I would pick as my most important asset the ability to concentrate. I worked hard at the discipline of concentration, constantly talking to myself at the crease to ensure that my attention did not wander. It is the one piece of advice I would pass on to any youngster who I thought was going to be any good — work at concentration.

The 1950s

GODFREY EVANS AND ALAN KNOTT AT WORK. During Godfrey Evans' last season, I used to wonder whether we would ever see his like again. How could anyone be a better wicketkeeper? Yet, within a year or two there appeared young Alan Knott, of similar build and attacking outlook. He is just approaching his peak and I believe there is every chance that he will be Godfrey Evans' equal.

WOOLLEY THE CHAMPION OF KENT. (*Kent Messenger*.) Frank Woolley in his 80th year delights the assembled company at the Kent Annual Dinner. His captain in the twenties, Lord Cornwallis, enjoys the reminiscences. My generation, who never had the luck to see him play, stand in awe of his amazing record, listen with wonder at his feats. Who could bear comparison to-day?

When GRAEME POLLOCK (*left*) and GARFIELD SOBERS (*right*) are in full flight I find it hard to believe that Frank Wooley could have been any better. They are both correct, strong and possess the attacking flair sufficient to disarm every bowler and any field a captain can set against them.

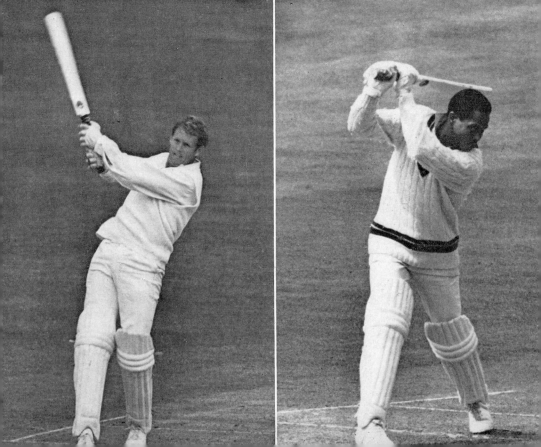

The 1950s

In 1950 I had a successful season for Tonbridge, as indeed I had the year before when I had scored 1,000 runs, played in both school matches at Lord's, caught and bowled Peter May for very few in the match against Combined Services and played for Kent second eleven without much distinction but apparently with enough skill to impress those who played alongside.

In July 1950 I was offered two games with the County during Maidstone week. It was term time and understandably the Headmaster refused me permission to play. In August I was given the chance of playing in four County matches. This time I accepted.

This was a time of change in English cricket. Despite a hiding from West Indies which was really brought about by the spin twins, Ramadhin and Valentine, we were beginning to re-emerge as a force. The suffering of the immediate post-war years was over; quickly shaping was perhaps the best England team in twenty years. In the game one or two very professional cricketers were establishing themselves. There was much criticism of the England performance, yet the Test Match displays did not properly reflect the County game which was steadily developing.

* * *

I played my first innings for Kent at Derby against Gladwin and Jackson. I knew of them by reputation although their faces were not recognisable to me. Gladwin stuck in my mind as the man who had produced the leg-bye which won a Test Match for England in South Africa, but about their cricket I was supremely naive. As I sat in my pads waiting to bat I had to ask another Kent player the names of the various cricketers. Because of television and the spotlight which is constantly focused on the players nowadays, no present-day youngster could go into the game as innocent as I was. It almost embarrasses me now to recall my first meeting with the great Bedser at Blackheath. If I had any thought about him as a bowler at all it was as someone who bowled straight, sometimes did something funny off the pitch and who knocked the sticks out of the ground if you missed him.

As soon as I faced up to him he bowled a half-volley wide of my off-stump. I started by aiming to drive it wide of mid-off when the ball began to swing into me. As I adjusted my stroke to hit the ball wide of mid-on I remember thinking with surprise "He bowls the in-swinger then". By the time I had finished adjusting my shot I hit the ball sweetly off the middle of the bat and was caught by Lock at backward short-leg...for nought. Today I would have been able to study all his tricks from behind his arm through the television eye.

One of my games was against the West Indians, unfortunately without Ramadhin, at Canterbury. The crowd was huge and for the first time as a participant I tasted the atmosphere of a big game. We had West Indies in trouble with half-a-dozen wickets gone cheaply, when Gerry Gomez scored a century. He was run out in the end by his partner, Prior Jones, who received such a blistering that he sat on his bat with tears streaming down his cheeks. On a wet wicket we were skittled out easily by Valentine with myself the top scorer, having played fairly well. I learnt how much there was for me to learn if I hoped to play for England.

* * *

Professionalism began to show in England's cricket during the 1950-51 tour of Australia. Once again we were defeated heavily, although much was made at the time of our winning the last Test — the first victory over Australia since the war. As an exercise in selection the party was inexplicable.

For one thing it contained six opening batsmen — Hutton, Washbrook, Simpson, Sheppard, Dewes and Parkhouse. Freddie Brown was the captain on the strength of a spectacular innings for the Gentlemen against the Players, and emerged as one of the side's heroes, making important runs and bowling more overs than anybody except Bedser. He was forty years old, yet with his attack falling apart around him, he bowled medium-paced seamers as well as his normal leg-breaks. It was a Union Jack performance from a great-hearted cricketer.

Yet the significant thing on the tour was the emergence of three professionals. Hutton had established himself as supreme with a Test average of eighty-eight, which was fifty runs better than the next man. Bedser, with no support, took thirty wickets. Evans, behind the stumps, was magnificent.

By 1951, my first full season in County cricket, I was aware of Hutton, Bedser and Evans as the three masters.

In 1952 Len Hutton was captain of England and the game had

already become fully professional. Peter May, amateur by virtue of being educated at Charterhouse and Cambridge but every bit as professional in method as Jack Hobbs, played his first Test against South Africa in 1951...Statham appeared as an important bowler... Trueman played against India...so did Lock...Laker re-established himself after his false start...Graveney went to India and scored hundreds at will in 1951-52.

You could feel the game toughening and tightening.

* * *

Sir Leonard Hutton can boast a magnificent record as England captain. Against the very strong West Indies team of 1953-54 in the Caribbean he held them to a level series and as captain won the Ashes at home in 1953 and away in 1954-55.

As a captain Len was a man you had to fit in with, but then that was probably true of most of the leading captains during his time as a player. Carr of Notts, Sellers — Hutton's own county captain — Jardine, Bradman, Hammond, one has heard tales of the idiosyncrasies of them all.

He had learned and played his cricket in the '30s when professionals took their orders and had to get on with it even if they didn't like it. From that background he suddenly found himself as the leader, issuing the orders but to post-war players of different philosophy. I am not sure he was ever fully able to adjust his outlook, and to make it harder for him, he was extremely conscious of being captain of England. It was a responsibility he never let himself escape for a moment.

To me he was an enormous help. He was interested in my play

with the result that I was prepared to put up with his curious form of leg-pulling to satisfy my hunger for information. When he liked you he could pass on tips about batting that you might not learn in a season at the crease. But you had to accept that he was going to help you in his own individual way.

He was at his best on the cricket field. As a captain he knew what it was all about — what the batsman did not want to face at any particular moment. Every change in bowling or field placing was made with the express purpose of squeezing the batsman. You felt that mentally he was that batsman, even though he may be standing at slip.

This may seem elementary, the basic job of all captains. Yet as far as I saw Len rarely got it wrong. It was impossible to fault him on bowling changes or field placing. If he had his life over again, I think he might want to be captain of a side younger, make his mistakes younger, learn the intracacies of handling his fellow players younger instead of having to gather this experience in the space of a Test Match day.

As a batsman there is a tendency by those who played with him to play him down a little, to qualify his claim to greatness by classing him as a fine technician. He was that, but he was also a very great opening batsman, perhaps one of the greatest there has ever been.

I say this from my only small experience of opening the innings in five Test Matches in West Indies when Wes Hall and Chester Watson were unleashing salvoes of bouncers. It was a time not to be an opening batsman.

On that basis it is interesting to think of the times when it was not the ideal time to be opening the innings in series between

England and Australia. 1921 would have been a good time to miss when Gregory and Macdonald were firing away at a poor England side. And nobody would want to have been in Fingleton's shoes in Australia in 1932.

But the longest period you could be forgiven for choosing to miss would have been that between 1946 and 1950 when Lindwall and Miller were operating with Johnston, Loxton and others in support. Yet as a result of the 1946, 1948 and 1950 series Hutton emerged as the best player of his time. Even after his one setback when he was dropped in 1948 he came back to score eighty-one and fifty-seven at Leeds and to be last man out when England were hurried out at the Oval. His batting in those four years was a triumph, especially when it is remembered that this was a personal war he was fighting for the fast bowling was directed at him as his side's most successful batsman, as it was being directed at no other player. Not only his skill but his courage was also under constant attack.

And 1953-54 in West Indies was probably a time not to be captain either. No longer a youngster, leading a side that lost the first two Test Matches, he achieved a marvellous performance. Mainly as a result of his batting the series was eventually drawn. At no time can Len be said to have had it easy, either as captain or batsman.

I have another reason to praise Hutton during this period. For much of the time he stood alone and it must be harder to be the only great player around. Admittedly, Cyril Washbrook played a very effective supporting role and they became a notable opening partnership.

A final word. What other batsman in the history of cricket has been subjected to the same array of great fast bowling over such a period as faced Hutton between 1946 and 1953? Not only did he come through unscathed, but he emerged the master.

The balance of power in the game had evened out. Whereas matches before 1953 were won by the side lucky enough to have fast bowlers — meaning Australia — from then onwards there were fast bowlers on almost every side. Sometimes Test Matches were more like artillery duels than games of cricket with the games being decided by the ability of one set of batsmen to hang on longer than the other.

In terms of sheer hostility Australia were probably worse served for fast bowlers at the start of the decade than most. Comparatively speaking that is, because Lindwall and Miller were still highclass new ball bowlers capable of making anybody think twice about opening the batting. Yet the edge had gone off their extreme speed and their later spells were inclined to be milder than in earlier days. They were in the second half of their careers.

England, for so long starved of fast bowlers, now positively bristled with them. Peter Loader, a really nasty fast bowler with an awkward change of pace and a well controlled slower ball, came to the fore.

Frank Tyson appeared and within five years had disappeared. For three years about his peak period although he played longer, he was the most savage thing in my experience. The question that intrigues me about him is the unanswerable one of how he compared with Harold Larwood. Certainly I would have put him ahead of Trueman, Statham and the rest of his contemporaries for speed and a thunderous strength which enabled him to blaze away at batsmen when by all the normal rules of human behaviour he should have been flagging. Threading his way through the entire decade and beyond was Brian Statham, the perfect fast bowler, equable of temperament and ever ready to do the labouring job of bowling into the wind without complaint. Surely no captain has had an easier cricketer to handle.

For South Africa there were Heine and Adcock, a belligerent pair. They tend to be forgotten by people in compiling a list of the most dangerous bowlers of that period, but the batsmen who played against them will always remember them. They would have figured large in the game, I think, had they played for England or Australia, teams with whom they would have got more cricket.

In 1957 there appeared in England Roy Gilchrist of West Indies, a brutal bowler, as fast as Tyson but suspect of action. A couple of years later an Indian, Desai, another with a loose action, proved quick and deceptive.

Then in West Indies in 1959–60 Wes Hall, a much gentler bowler when he bowled with Gilchrist in England, demonstrated his ability as a man of genuine pace. In all five Tests he opened the bowling and I opened the batting. He had Chester Watson, a willing user of the new ball as his partner and the experience was spiteful. With the ball seldom played less than chest high, my partner, Geoff Pullar, was magnificent. He had a model temperament and a good technique. I shall never quite understand how or why he slipped off the top rung. By the end of that tour Hall's next partner, Charlie Griffith, had appeared. With his doubtful action he was able to generate enormous speed and in 1963, on a slow Leeds wicket, as five Englishmen went for a few runs, he was to bowl viciously quick. I watched it from the television commentary box having had my arm broken earlier in the series, and wondered.

Meanwhile Australia had found a second wave of fast bowlers

producing two men whom we euphemistically describe as having suspect actions in Meckiff and Rorke, backed by Alan Davidson, that comparative rarity — a quick left-hander.

To grade this collection of the world's fast bowlers is next to impossible. It is easy to ask who was the best I played against, but less easy to answer for they possessed between them so many differing qualities. The only way I can give a real impression of my rating of them is to divide them into three categories.

The most awkward to play were the throwers, the men of "suspect actions". The technical difficulties of batting against them are well enough known not to need repeating here. Happily, I believe we have solved the problem and we shall not see a throwing plague again in my lifetime.

In order of awkwardness:—

1. Gilchrist.
2. Griffith.
3. Meckiff.

The most skilful I played against:—

1. Lindwall.
2. Trueman.
3. Bedser (who does not really belong in this analysis of fast bowlers as he was really fast-medium, but who had so much talent that it is impossible to survey the bowling scene without including him).

Of the fastest, the men who relied solely on their speed:—

1. Tyson.
2. Hall.
3. Statham.

For six overs of the new ball:—

1. Davidson.
2. Sobers.

43

* * *

The leading English batsman during these years of violence was Peter May. It may well have been also that he was the best player in the world at that time. To give some idea of his skill, I have considered other players with whom to compare him and find it completely impossible. He was not like Hutton or Compton, two men who were the top players of their period. In fact he was not like anybody except Peter May, either in character or method.

Off the field he was a quietly-spoken, mild-mannered man, self-effacing and rather diffident. At the crease he changed character becoming a person who bristled with defiance, belligerence and suspicion. I cannot recall that in all the times we batted together he actually snorted fire, but he should have done.

As a student of games I found this transformation intriguing. It was the opposite, for instance, of the top golfers whose aim is to relax and keep down the tempo within themselves. It was alien to my own approach to batting which encompasses the occasional chat and even more occasional laugh while at the crease combined with an interest in all that is going on.

Happily, we enjoyed batting together and can look back on quite a number of crucial partnerships. I treasure this enormously.

He was not master of what I call "touch", so that he seldom cut and never played the more delicate deflections, but he square cut savagely and whipped off his toes better than anyone. He had immense strength.

In terms of pure skill he had less than some players who have achieved less. I am thinking particularly of Ted Dexter who I have seen play some innings which I am convinced could not have been bettered. But May had the mental ability to give everything to every battle. It is a rare gift and in the end he became drained by it.

But it made him a very great player.

* * *

There have been two Tom Graveneys in cricket. It is the only explanation I can produce for his rather unfortunate stop-go Test career. For a man of his talent — and I put him fourth in the list of England's best batsmen after Hutton, Compton and May — he played relatively little Test cricket between 1953 and 1966. Yet from 1966 when he came back against West Indies at the age of thirty-nine he was quite incomparable.

There must have been a difference between the first Graveney and the second. Reason says it, figures say it, for in the end it is the size of a man's figures which decides whether he stays in the team or not — and he's said it himself. If you keep scoring runs it is impossible to drop you. An inquiry into his career, closer than I am able to conduct here, might well serve as a guide to today's emerging stroke players.

He started as a natural player, which may have rebounded on him in the early stages of his career. Possibly it took him to the top too quickly before he had time to fill in all the holes in his technique. Test cricket is a desperately hard place to repair even one fault.

Probably too, he did not find it easy applying himself to Test Matches in those days and might have found it hard to lift his play a little in the way that Test cricket demands. Remember, when talking of his faults he first played for Gloucestershire in

1948 and yet for England in 1951. It was not a long apprenticeship.

Perhaps the point can best be made by imagining a crisis in a Test Match with Graveney, the brilliant attacking player that he was of the 1950s, going out to face it with a more mature but less talented Ken Barrington. Ken, I feel sure, would have been more able to raise himself to the demands. But in Graveney all this changed. When he came back in 1966 he was the complete player – steady, determined, faultless. His success in Test cricket speaks for itself, but some of his performances for Worcestershire on bad pitches were above anything the rest of us could have done.

It gives hope for us all that at thirty-nine he was definitely a better player than he had been before. With it all he was a tremendous accumulator of runs. It was plain he wanted them every time he went to the wicket, a trait in him I admire and envy. Graveney, playing a country side in Ceylon, would go for the hundred once he had established himself, and get real enjoyment from it, whereas for myself thirty or forty would be enough unless I were out of form or practising something new. I would need to have a reason to go on. With Tom the sheer joy of batting is enough.

Over the years he has been a great ornament to the top class game. Spotlessly turned out, keen in the field and so attractive in his batting that even his struggles have elegance, I doubt if any other player has consistently given so much pleasure.

* * *

Richie Benaud wrote his name deeply into the Test cricket of his time very early on in his career. From the start he had two great assets — talent and a superb athleticism. Moreover, he had that indefinable quality which not all great players have, of personality. Somehow, he caught the eye, even if he was not playing well.

He had, in my opinion, probably the most unusually nervous temperament of any young Australian cricketer and this threatened his future as a player. It seems odd now when he is such a sophisticated serene man to talk of him as being immature for an Australian, but his nervousness in those early days was startling to see.

As a result he never broke through into Test Cricket (and in fact, never looked like doing it) until it seemed that he was ready to be written off as a failure, or at best a half-success. After the 1954-55 and 1956 series against England he was no nearer establishing himself than he had been before they started. In 1956 the person he troubled most in the England side was myself mainly because I was going through an odd phase in my batting as well. The talk at the time was that Australia in Benaud, Davidson and Archer were overstocked with bits and pieces players whereas England were achieving their success through specialist players. All three were recognised as useful first-class cricketers without having the extra 'edge' to turn them into Test players. Except in the case of Ron Archer, who was forced out of the game through injury, it was proved that this was just another piece of wrong guessing.

For Benaud, I think, must twice have been close to disappearing from the game. The first time was after the 1956 tour of England, a crisis he faced and beat on Australia's long tour of the following Winter which took in South Africa. I can only guess how hard he worked at his bowling on that trip, but by the time I faced him

47

again during M.C.C.'s 1958-59 visit he had changed from an ordinary bowler into a specialist. He had learned the flipper, he had learned more variations, he had better control, and was more sure of himself.

From that moment he progressed. He was made captain of Australia and from the dual roles of player and leader he gathered the success and the prestige which have been the driving power of his cricket. He had something to live up to and he proceeded to live up to it. Time and again Meckiff and Davidson gave him the break-through and he picked up the rest of the wickets. In that series he took thirty-one wickets. He faltered again in England in 1961, not so much because of his bowling, although he was never such a good bowler here as overseas, but more because of his health.

He was troubled for most of the summer by an injured shoulder and half way through the tour he was clearly depressed. He missed the Second Test at Lord's which Australia won under Neil Harvey and came back for the Third which England won and in which he scored a pair and took only two wickets. Had England won at Manchester, which seemed likely, he might have found his position as captain in jeopardy. Instead, in an hour, from the moment Dexter's great innings ended, the game changed dramatically and he won the match for Australia.

Once he became captain he seemed to have control over his temperament without losing any of his exuberance. He was inspired I think by the suffering he personally, and the side had suffered firstly, from Len Hutton in 1954-55, and then from Jim Laker in 1956. They left him with debts to pay and he paid them all off against the 1958 England team, which on paper at least, was one of the most formidable parties ever to go on tour. Benaud beat us in the royal manner, four-nil.

Probably because of his association with journalism, he established himself as a publicist captain, ever ready to receive and answer the questions of the Press. He did the job successfully and he became a very popular figure, yet there was no question of self-glorification in it. He was conscious of the need to promote cricket in Australia at a time when the public had become disillusioned by lack of success. He was then, and still is devoted to the game and I have a high regard for his judgement.

* * *

When we sailed to Australia in 1958-59, I recall trying to evaluate the strength of our side. We were very strong indeed, and maybe Peter May had one of the best sides that ever left these shores. Bowling has always been the key in Test Matches and the presence of Trueman, Statham, Tyson, Loader, Bailey, Laker and Lock seemed a combination which could not feature on the losing side under any conditions that could be imagined. Godfrey Evans was still behind the wicket and a nucleus of May, Cowdrey, Graveney and Watson (an under-estimated player if ever there was one) suggested that whatever the calibre of our opening batsmen, we were going to take some bowling out. In fact, Richardson and Milton, the selected openers, were two very fine players with considerable success behind them.

But there were two factors which no one could have predicted. This was the tour when "throwing" reared its ugly head in a big way. Unless you played through it, as I did, it would be impossible to understand quite what a problem it presented. Maybe we played badly, but even so, largely because of the unpredictability of the throw, we never got a start to any innings until the Fourth Test Match. The throwers were at their most awkward of course when the new ball was taken with its hardness and bounce. Their influence on the games is best illustrated by England's first innings in the Second Test at Melbourne. The first three wickets fell for seven runs and the fourth at forty-two. Peter May and I took the score to 210, when with the second new ball, Meckiff had Peter May's stump in a whirl before Peter had completed his backlift. In a trice, it seemed, we were all out for 259, just when it looked as if we were going to build up a useful score. I felt very sorry for both Richardson and Milton, whose Test careers became clouded by their failure at the hands of these throwers.

The second major factor was the sudden and quite dramatic demise of Tony Lock. Those who have seen and admired him in recent years, whether bowling for Leicestershire or Western Australia, would find it hard to picture him failing as he did in the '50s. Derek Underwood is constantly under fire for bowling too quick for a slow bowler, but he is leisurely compared with the Lock aggression, as he dragged and threw, cutting the ball off the indifferent English surfaces at a pace much akin to Alec Bedser's leg-cutters. In England he could be unplayable and no one will ever know how Laker got nineteen wickets at Manchester, whilst Tony Lock battled away from the other end, beating the bat with great regularity, but with so little to show for it. In Australia he had to alter and he could not settle on the right rhythm. He tried quick and he tried very slow, he tried everything — for Tony Lock, without exception, is the greatest trier I have ever seen on a cricket field. Alas, he lost confidence and that, from Peter May's point of view, was a disaster.

We got off to a bad start, as we usually do at Brisbane. Although we went into the next Test determined to put things right and determined, too, to try not to let the throwing problem affect us overmuch, it seemed we just could not get a footing. The same thing so often happens at games if you once let up in a match in which you are clearly superior. When it comes to having to tighten the screw again, the opposition have their tails up and it is not so easy to get on terms. Once the tour started to slide, Peter May was under tremendous pressure and try as he did, he could not hold it. On paper we were the better side but on the field with the passes and the breaks eluding us, the Australians put in the better performance and deserved to win. It was a humiliating defeat, almost as total as that of Bill Lawry's team in South Africa last Winter. In contrast, Jack Cheetham's South African side had just left Australia and were something of an ordinary side on paper, but it surprised everyone by drawing the series.

This had been a supreme example of team effort. This is the sort of thing that we see more and more in British sport. Our best English football is notable for this at the moment and our success in West Indies two years ago would not have been possible but for it. It is a lesson I have learned. You can have all the stars in the world but there is nothing more stimulating than to be a member of a team who will give everything they have to the team's success. It is even more moving if you are lucky enough, as I was, to be captain. I think this is the greatest fun that cricket can bring.

* * *

Why was it that the army of throwers appeared in the late 1950s and early 1960s? It was not as if one country suddenly found them as the means for achieving success. They were international. Everybody had them.

As with almost everything else that has gone wrong with cricket, the conditions which were to produce them, may have sprung, I believe, from the change in the lbw law in 1935. I talked earlier of the revolution in bowling which resulted after the war with bowlers shortening the length of their bowling to counter the forward defensive stroke.

The next development was to drag the back foot as they strove to become more precise in their aim. The area they were aiming at — just short enough of a length to prevent their being driven — was comparatively small and to cut out error they tried to get closer to the batsman before releasing the ball.

Clearly it is awkward to keep the arm in a vertical position half way through the delivery action while the foot is dragging. There was a tendency for the elbow to collapse a little and for the arm to crinkle. The result was a throw. It was no coincidence that most of the throwers were draggers.

Before Meckiff and Rorke lacerated England in the 1958 series there was not much preoccupation with throwers. They were about, of course. I had played against Cuan McCarthy of South Africa in the 'Varsity match, and his quicker and suspect delivery was very quick, but until the mid-'50s there had been no successful throwers, and so nobody cared much about them. They were despised in a way because they offended the classical idea. They had ugly actions, they could not bowl straight, etc. When they arrived in strength their inaccuracy proved to be one of their strengths. The first ball

Meckiff bowled to Arthur Milton in the Brisbane Test went for four byes down the leg side. The next went straight at first-slip. The third knocked his stumps over. For the batsmen facing the throwers in that series there were about two balls an over to play at. You never felt that you were building an innings simply because you never saw enough of the ball.

It would hurtle past, yards wide, for minutes on end and just when you had started to lose patience and mutter to yourself that this was ridiculous, you would get the straight one. The result was that with bowling lacking any kind of control or virtue other than it was unpunishable, the throwers would turn in bowling figures that would have been proudly owned by the men of highest skill. Meckiff's figures for the two innings of the First Test at Brisbane (and remember they were eight ball overs) were 17-5-33-3 and 19-7-30-2.

The real debate about throwers started gradually. Lock's quick ball caused much questioning and though I did not see it as a throw at the time retrospectively I can accept it as such. There was talk too, of Loader's bouncer and of Gilchrist, who delivered the ball from wide of the crease which is the sign of all throwers.

Once the size of the problem was seen and the threat it posed to the whole game appreciated, the clean-up followed quickly. Nobody was more thorough than Australia, led by a militant Sir Donald Bradman. Notwithstanding that they had more throwers than any other country they got rid of them more quickly than anybody else. Four years after 1958 when M.C.C. returned, there was not a thrower to be seen. This reflects great credit on the Australian Board of Control.

Tony Lock, who figured in the drama of throwing, brought

about his own reformation, beginning after being shocked at the sight of himself on a film shown midway through a match in New Zealand. From that moment on he started to look for a new bowling method while we, who were playing for a day off in the game, fumed while he bowled little "droppers" that kept us at our posts. However much we would have liked him to postpone his reforming for another twenty-four hours, there can be nothing but admiration for the success he has made of the job. He has again established himself as one of the world's leading slow left-handers and become a power in the Sheffield Shield. That in itself is an irony when one considers that had he been bowling in 1958 as he is now, England's attack would have been more formidable.

* * *

If I had to nominate an entry for a competition to find cricket's most brilliant selection, I would go for that of Sonny Ramadhin as a member of the West Indies party of 1950. Without any batting or fielding ability and with only a handful of wickets to his credit, he was pulled out of club cricket in Trinidad to become the destroyer of England. It was a most fantastic piece of crystal-ball gazing on the part of the selectors. He had, of course, a snappy bowling action which produced off-breaks and occasionally leg-breaks without enough change to tell the batsmen which was coming. English batsmen, that is. Everton Weekes was amazed at the inability of Hutton, Washbrook, Compton and the rest to read Ramadhin's spin and he went into every match certain that this was the one in which the mystery was to be solved. He claimed that in the nets all the West Indies party could tell which way he was turning the ball.

54

But that year the English batsmen never did find the answer. I watched Cyril Washbrook score a hundred in the Test Match at Lord's and it was as clear at the end as it had been at the beginning, that he could not read the spin.

Ramadhin in that first meeting with England was sharper and quicker than when I played against him. By then he had taken savage punishment in Australia and the fine edge had gone off his bowling. Even so he was still dangerous enough to be the subject of some special thinking when we opened the 1957 series at Edgbaston.

The Australians had destroyed him by attacking him and we opted for a similar method stupidly forgetting that in Australia Ramadhin would not have turned the ball. In effect the opposite happened and had rain finished the match after our first innings I think we might have been competing with a Ramadhin bogey throughout the series. We chose the wrong place to be aggressive. The pitch at Edgbaston lacks the pace or the bounce to make it an acceptable policy, with the result that we were dismissed for 186 with Ramadhin taking seven for forty-nine. In the second innings we decided simply to play him and Peter May and myself put on over 400. We never mastered him but by the end we were reading him without trouble.

Even without his magic he might still have been an influence on the series because he was never less than a good bowler, but the next match finished him. He had to do his share of bowling on a grassy Lord's wicket on which a spinner would never have got to the bowling crease in a county match and on which Shackleton or Cartwright would have been unmanageable. By the end of that match he was very depressed.

He tried a spell with Lancashire and it was a measure of how far he had deteriorated since I saw him bewildering Washbrook that he failed. On his 1950 form he would have raced to a hundred wickets every season in County cricket.

Probably because of tiredness he finished a shadow of himself and with rather a suspect action. He faded out of the first-class game. Had he been successful I think the umpires might have come down on him for it was widely known that his arm was offending. As it was they showed mercy. Whatever the letter of the law, I had no argument with them in his particular case.

* * *

For all the legendary success of the three Ws — Weekes, Worrell and Walcott — I shall always be rather sorry that they all came from the same little island, Barbados, at the same time. Ideally they should have been spread out a little more bringing their skill and their talent to entertain to a wider circle of players and spectators.

As it was they tended to overshadow each other. Each took a little from the other and they must have been victims of the same kind of pressure that McCabe had batting behind Bradman. On their own they might have been even more astonishing.

They are linked together now forever, yet there was nothing similar about their play. Worrell was a touch player, a man who used the pace of the ball. He was a beautiful deflector of the ball and he played the way I would like to play.

Walcott struck massively through the line. The sheer ferocity of his straight hitting off either front or back foot and his square cutting linger in the mind.

Of the three, Weekes struck me as the shrewdest. He too, was a dictator at the crease and with him there was always the impression that he was one move ahead of the bowler. He seemed to read the bowler's mind almost as well as he read his hand.

In the end, of course, Worrell became Sir Frank and gathered even more fame as a captain than he had as a batsman. He figured in one of the smoothest and most civilised captaincy change-overs that any cricket has known – and I speak not without authority on this subject! When England left West Indies at the end of the 1959–60 tour, I doubt if there was one of our players who did not think he had seen the last of Frank Worrell in Test cricket. He looked a jaded cricketer – "over the hill", to use an Australian expression, but in no time at all, he had taken over the side in Australia, and Gerry Alexander who had been his captain against England, had slipped quietly and without rancour into the position of vice-captain. There came the tied match at Brisbane and within a few months Frank Worrell was reestablished as a God-like figure in the game.

To us who had played against him and seen him struggle it came as something of a surprise. It should not have done for there is a recurring theme of unpredictability in cricket which makes all things possible. Had Freddie Brown scored a good thirty in the Gentleman and Players match in 1950 he would have made no mark on the history of the game. As it was he played a big innings and took the England side to Australia as captain. Had Roger Prideaux and Barry Knight not become casualties just before the last Test of 1968, Basil D'Oliveira would not have been brought back to score his first century against Australia and so on.

* * *

The fairly quick death of the leg-spinner was another result of the advent of poorer pitches and the seam bowler. Once Eric Hollies had left Warwickshire there was not another wrist-spinner good enough to command long term attention from selection committees realistically considering the economic worth of this type of bowler. They looked down the averages and saw that seam bowlers exploited bad conditions just as successfully as leg-spinners and at far less cost.

Surrey emphasised the point by winning the County Championship seven times without calling on a wrist-spinner. They were no longer necessary and so a wayward but exciting branch of the game withered.

Almost every county had a wrist-spinner at one time, including Yorkshire, who, despite a publicly expressed scorn of them, picked Eddie Leadbeater. But the game was already well on the change by 1957, my first year as captain of Kent. We were concerned at losing Doug Wright because he had been a magnificent bowler, but there was not the urgent thinking about replacing him that there would have been had he been a fast bowler or finger spinner of similar quality. It was more a case of covering the gap in quality rather than in kind.

Don Bradman brought Ring and McCool to England in 1948 and hardly used them. Freddie Brown was picked to bowl leg-breaks under Len Hutton at Lord's in 1953. Tommy Greenhough appeared spasmodically, Bob Barber bowled the occasional spell — these are men who are remembered because they are exceptions to the rule of the day. In this select company the most dangerous was Johnny

Wardle, an orthodox slow left-hander who also bowled out of the back of the hand.

The irony was that once wrist-spinners were dropped out of the county game as being unsuitable for English conditions, they were obviously not available to bowl on overseas pitches just the circumstances when England could have made use of them.

* * *

It was the misfortune of the first half of my international career to be seen as an opening batsman. I opened the innings in every match of three series against Australia, West Indies and South Africa and cannot recall having had less enjoyment from cricket in all my life.

It took the edge off the fun for me and I am one who by nature must get enjoyment from the game or else there is nothing. I can truthfully say that the only times I have woken up in the morning and not joyfully anticipated the day ahead was when I was opening the innings in a Test Match.

You have got to have a burning ambition to do this job to be any good at it. That was the point the selectors and my critics missed when they tried to make me into an opener. All the good opening batsmen I know would not bat anywhere else and feel rather sorry for middle order batsmen.

After that, on the occasions when I was selected to open the innings it was generally on the grounds of expediency. It was seen as the way of accommodating five middle order batsmen who were competing for four places. There was never any chance of my working up any enthusiasm for the task simply because the only time I ever did it was when I played for England. We already had two good established opening batsmen at Kent in Fagg and Phebey, and it would have been neither fair nor reasonable to have sent one of them down the order simply because I was hungry to play for England and wanted to take practice against the new ball at their expense.

Apart from the psychological requirements, the technical needs are pretty exacting too. Before the war it was undoubtedly a less complicated job than it is now in England. And on some overseas wickets like India, where the pitches have no pace and the ball has no shine after three overs, any competent member of the side is capable of doing it, but the first eighty minutes at Hove with the ball hopping about and jumping off the seam are a different proposition.

The essential need is for a man capable of disciplining himself and limiting his ambition. By 2.30 p.m. it is a different game. There is time enough for stroke-makers then.

* * *

It is interesting to link Compton and Bedser and two masters of their period if only because they prove what contrasting virtues go towards making a top-class cricketer. They had absolutely nothing in common.

Compton was carefree to the point that it was rare for him to go on to the field wearing only his own gear (invariably he had borrowed something from somebody else); gay, so that there was almost always some good-hearted confusion going on around him; and blessed with a flair that in 1947, and on many other occasions afterwards, amounted to genius.

Alec, by contrast, was a quiet, studious man of tremendous courage and determination. If in the light of Compton's flamboyance he sounds dull, the impression is wrong. He was certainly single-minded about cricket, yet he was blessed with a sense of humour which, if it seldom allowed him to make a joke never stopped him from appreciating one. Of the two it was predictable that Bedser would rise to a position of authority within the game and he has done that by becoming chairman of the Test selection committee.

The appointment gave him extra pleasure, I believe, in view of his place in the game as a bowler. He is not slow to tell anyone that cricket belongs to batsmen and that bowlers are the labourers. — "The last bowler to get knighted was Sir Francis Drake" I've heard him say. In his case that was particularly true for as I said earlier he was the only quick bowler of class of his time. No modern cricketer can have shed as much sweat in England's cause as he did. Still the sheer labour of those days may have been his making. I have a theory that the astronomical number of overs he bowled against the heaviest scoring batsmen in the game and the dedication he applied to it made him into the outstanding English bowler of his time. He literally worked his way to the top.

His figures against Australia support the theory. In the 1946-47 series he took sixteen wickets at a cost of fifty-four runs each while the Australian batting averages had a dreamlike quality about them with Bradman sitting at the top with ninety-seven, and Hassett with forty-seven, as low as sixth. They strike me as being the ordinary figures of an ordinary good bowler.

The pattern for the 1948 series was different with Bedser taking eighteen wickets at thirty-eight apiece. By then Bradman was talking of him as the best fast-medium bowler he had seen since Maurice Tate. The truth of that comparison was made plain between 1948 and 1954 and if it were possible to draw a line on players of different eras it might well prove that he was a better bowler than Tate. Certainly he would have been a shrewder one. In 1950, in a poor England side, he arrived in the top class with thirty Australian wickets in the series. Admittedly Bradman had gone by then, but Hassett, Harvey, Morris, Burke and Miller were playing yet the most successful Australian batsman, Miller, averaged only forty-three.

The figures show the developing power of Bedser. If sheer hard work were the inspiration then Bedser would be the last to deny it for as a man concerned in building a successful business since he left cricket, he has a natural suspicion of anything that comes easy. He might well envy the present-day seam bowler the pitches he has to bowl on compared with those of his own day, but in his heart too, he is sure that the ease with which they are able to succeed makes them lesser bowlers.

The danger in talking about Compton after that is that any reference to the high spirits and zest that were the hallmarks of his cricket might be interpreted as a charge of flippancy. No man could play as unforgettably as him without a hard apprenticeship at the basics of batting. The difference with Compton, say from Hutton, was that you would never have suspected how much work had gone into his play.

In that year of 1947 by which he will always be remembered, he skipped up and down the pitches of England playing quick bowlers as if they were slow bowlers with strokes so far removed from the ordinary that he seemed to invent them during the backlift. It was a marvellous game he played, the golden boy in a golden year. Keeping him company most of the time was Edrich, small and pugnacious, whose own huge success somehow seemed to cast even more glory on Compton, yet beneath the gaiety in Compton and the enjoyment he clearly derived from entertaining, there was a serious side. He would fight in a crisis as hard as anybody, and if the innings he played against Australia at Manchester in 1948 is the one most commonly cited to make the point, then it is surely the best. He was led off the field with England thirty-two for two having been hit on the head hooking at a Lindwall bouncer. He came back, sporting two stitches and looking like the survivor of a road accident, at 119 for five. He stayed in all five and a half hours and scored 145.

* * *

The phenomenon of the 1950s was Peter Richardson. Most Test opening batsmen can be seen from a long way off. They seem to graduate with honours at each level of the game so that it is almost impossible to mistake their pedigree. Richardson was different. He suddenly seemed to thrust his way into the ranks of the international players when he played in all five Test Matches against Australia in 1956, his only experience of representative cricket having been a tour of Pakistan the previous winter. And with all respect to the cricketers of Pakistan of whom there are very many good ones, a tour of that country with its bias towards batsmen has never been regarded as conclusive.

Richardson arrived at a time when I was having one of my enforced spells of opening the innings for England. He was a joy to bat with and this experience forged a friendship. From what I remember, he was a long way from being an automatic choice. Don Kenyon was Richardson's partner for Worcestershire and I have no doubt in my own mind who most people would have named as the England batsman had they seen the pair batting together. Kenyon in county cricket was a very impressive player.

Jack Robertson, a fine player who unluckily had to wait in the wings behind Hutton and Washbrook, was still around. So was Reg Simpson. Neither of them was exactly youthful nor represented an investment for the future, but when Australia have been the opponents birth certificates have tended not to come into the reckoning. Experience has usually been the decisive quality.

Frank Lowson who in his earlier days had been freely tipped as Hutton's successor, was playing for Yorkshire; Sussex had Don Smith, and Alan Oakman and Maurice Hallam was going strongly for Leicestershire. There was certainly enough opposition about for the choice of Richardson to be questioned.

It worked out right though and he set up one of the quickest times for reaching a 1,000 runs in Test cricket. Yet before the 1950s were out the Test game had already started to go against him. In the best of conditions he would probably have found it taxing to adapt his technique to the extra pace and bounce of Australian pitches, but the throwers killed him and his enthusiasm.

In a party doubtful about the reliability of the opening batting, he was the only established player. In theory he was supposed to hold one end while the selectors permutated his partners at the other. In the event he scored 162 runs in eight innings. Whatever the final mishaps in his career as a Test player, there is no doubt that Richardson justified his repeated selection. He had a serene temperament, a good cricket intelligence, and the self-discipline to play within his limitations. He was a superb runner between the wickets.

These limitations in his England days were based on a backlift of no measurable movement and an insatiable appetite for deflections and pushes mainly in the area square of the wicket. By the time he finished with Kent he was a quite different player — a full blooded stroke maker and a unique sweeper of the ball sometimes playing extravagant shots with both feet off the ground. It had been a remarkable transformation.

* * *

There can never be a simple explanation of what made Trevor Bailey a leading cricketer, or how is was that he could regularly bring such despair into the lives of far more gifted players on the other side so that they would frequently finish the day in need of psychiatric treatment.

The public saw him as a fighter and in this they were right, which is somewhat unusual, for the public have an uncanny knack of misreading the characters of their favourite sportsmen. With Bailey, of whom it was once said that he always went to the crease prepared to create a crisis if there was not one already in existence, there could be no mistaking his complete absorption in a fight.

This is, I think, the story of his life. Even away from the field he revels in competing against the odds. He is the man who would take the local council all the way through to the High Court for not emptying his dustbin...probably he looked with awe on the bus passenger in Hampshire who staged his own go-slow and stopped the bus at request stops so that he could admire the scenery.

He started his cricket life as a tearaway fast bowler, one of those slaughtered when Bradman's side made 700 in a day against Essex.

He was useful but short of the highest class and he really only made a mark at all because there were no quick bowlers about at the time. It is hard to see that he would have gone very far. Apart from anything else, fast bowling with its comparative lack of sophistication would hardly have fitted in with his nature. For him it was a good day when the crop of genuine fast bowlers appeared. The advent of Trueman, Statham, Tyson and the rest enabled him to drop his pace and become a very fine, accurate medium-pace bowler. He may not have possessed the ability to be a lead bowler for England, but he was ideally cast for the role of support bowler. Yet to be a key member of the best England side of modern times he had to do more than bowl. He had to be able to field and to bat well enough to fill the all-rounder position in a side so top heavy with bowling specialists that it was even more important than usual. On both the fielding and the batting counts he baffled me.

He was not cut out by nature to be a good fielder for he was not a natural mover and he had very brittle fingers which were broken more than most. Yet he took catches in Test Matches to equal anything produced by the Benauds and Simpsons of this world. In the mind's eye I can see him diving flat out across the ground from slip to take a catch one-handed with the arm so extended that it seemed it must come out of the socket.

Then there was his batting. As a batsman myself who studied his method over the years with growing disbelief I can only say that is was very pawky, yet constantly as England searched desperately for an opening batsman to stave off some temporary

FRANK TYSON at top speed in the Fourth Test match at Adelaide in 1955 under the eye of his captain, Len Hutton, at mid-on. He was the outstanding man of the series and was the central figure in bringing back the Ashes.

THE BENT ARM PLAGUE OF THE FIFTIES. These five shots of Ian Meckiff of Australia show the bones of the problem and give some idea of the advantage gained. Gordon Rourke (*left*) of Australia, too, was a frightening proposition to bat against. This picture shows the open chest which is part and parcel of the complaint. R. Gilchrist (*bottom right*), West Indies, in this picture is just about to open out and splay his front foot towards the gully. His fast bouncer and yorker were terrifying. Tony Lock (*above right*), once of Surrey and England but more recently of Leicestershire and Western Australia has been a unique case. As a youngster he was a genuine slow bowler who used the air in orthodox fashion. On the bad wickets of the fifties he learned to drag and throw. By 1960, he had taken a year out to re-model his action and since has become a very fine slow bowler indeed.

SIR LEONARD HUTTON upon whom fell the brunt of Lindwall and Miller in the post-war years. He came through this torrid battering supreme. We tend to forget what a complete player he was who, when the situation arose, could destroy the spinners as decisively as most.

RAY LINDWALL OF AUS-TRALIA AT THE CLIMAX BEFORE DELIVERY. He was the scourge of England batsmen from 1946-1956 and was the best bowler I have played against.

1. The late cut.

MY SEVEN FAVOURITE SHOTS

. Stroking the ball right of cover's left hand off the back foot. (*Sport and General*)

3. Forcing hard off the back foot through extra cover.

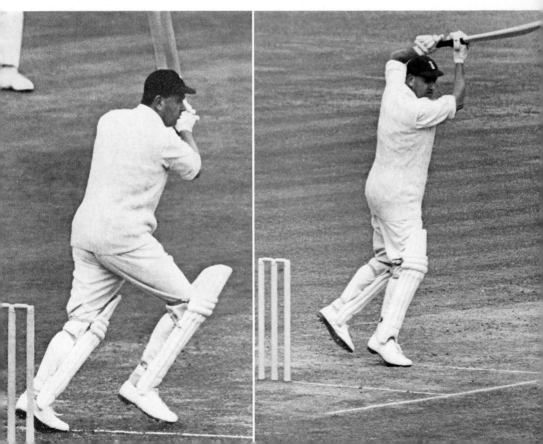

4. A strong right hand guides the short ball wide of mid-on.

5. The greatest thrill of all – cover driving.

6. Lofting the off-spinner over mid-on.

7. My version of the sweep.

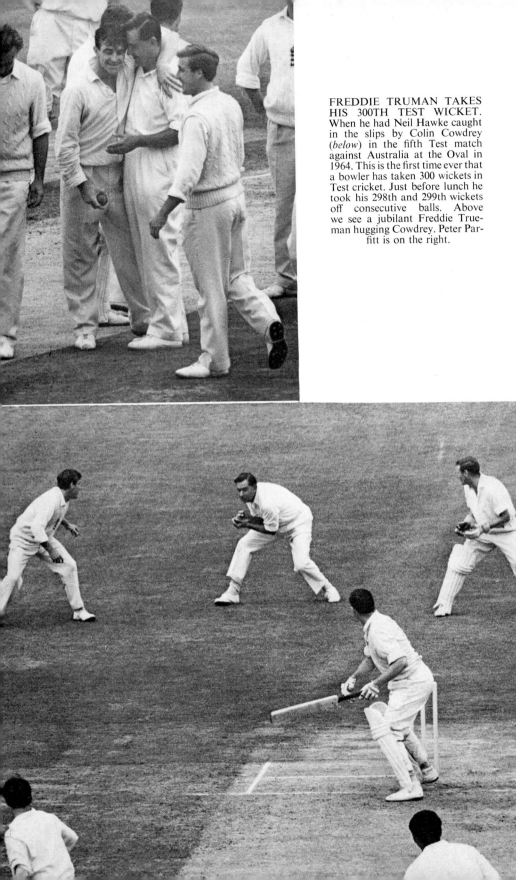

FREDDIE TRUMAN TAKES HIS 300TH TEST WICKET. When he had Neil Hawke caught in the slips by Colin Cowdrey (*below*) in the fifth Test match against Australia at the Oval in 1964. This is the first time ever that a bowler has taken 300 wickets in Test cricket. Just before lunch he took his 298th and 299th wickets off consecutive balls. Above we see a jubilant Freddie Trueman hugging Cowdrey. Peter Parfitt is on the right.

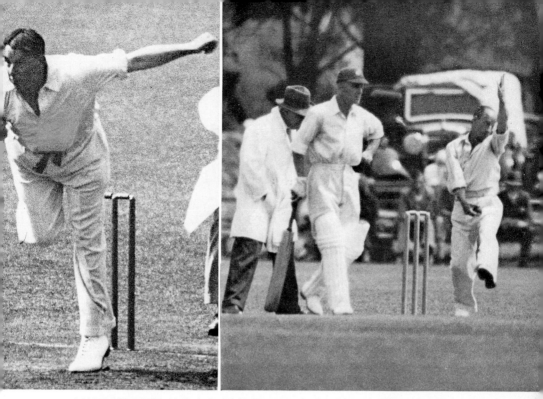

MAURICE TATE AND A. P. (Tich) FREEMAN. (*Radio Times Hulton Picture Library*.) I have the greatest admiration for these two bowlers, although I never actually saw them in action. The best bowlers of the day had the highest respect for them and their records speak for themselves. Maurice Tate's greatest years were before the change of the lbw law. How much greater a bowler he would have been with the new law to help him. Tich Freeman took 1100 wickets in 4 years – a feat that will never be surpassed. I count myself fortunate to have come to know them both very well in their retirement years. I spent hours listening to them talk cricket.

ROBIN HOBBS is the most experienced leg spinner in England, a brilliant fielder, a great trier and the perfect team man. He has had to learn to bowl defensively so as to keep his place in the Essex side on the many grassy wickets which we have to-day – a situation which, on his own admission, Tich Freeman rarely knew. Consequently, Robin Hobbs is still short of sufficient spin to have commanded an automatic place in the England side. Hobbs can take comfort from the fact that most of the great slow bowlers have been at their best after the age of thirty.

THE TWO RICHARDSONS. Peter Richardson. On the left we view the basis of his game for Worcestershire and England. He scored 1000 runs in Test cricket in fewer innings than anyone else. On the right we see the attacking Richardson of later years for Kent, not quite so effective in terms of reward, maybe, yet more entertaining and a truer reflection of his personality. (*Press Association*)

WEST INDIES RETURN. Thanks to a wonderful team effort, the captain was able to stride from the plane at London Airport with head held high and a beaming smile after victory in the West Indies, 1968. But for Jeff Jones's (of Glamorgan) batting in that last over at Georgetown . . . ! So often the fate of a match or series can hang on a slender thread – in this case, one over. (*Press Association*)

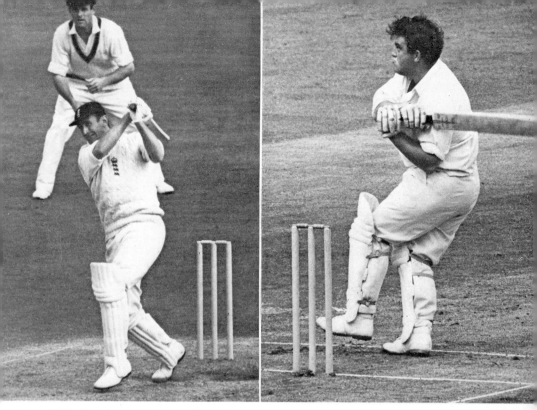

E. R. DEXTER drives furiously. I recall particularly his two innings at Brisbane in 1962 and his 70 against West Indies at Lords in 1963. Here was true greatness.

COLIN MILBURN in typical attacking vein. He was just producing his best when tragedy struck.

KEITH FLETCHER (ESSEX) AND JOHN HAMPSHIRE (YORKSHIRE) are fine cricketers who should be filling our middle order in the years ahead.

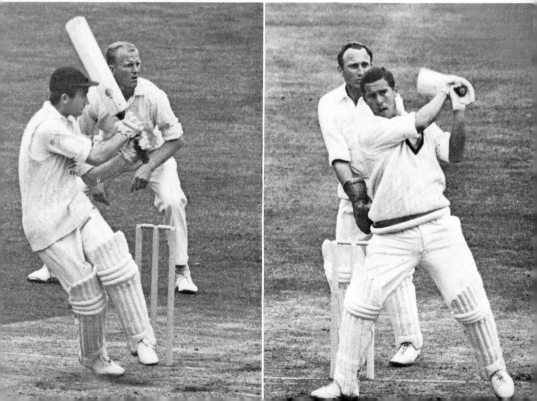

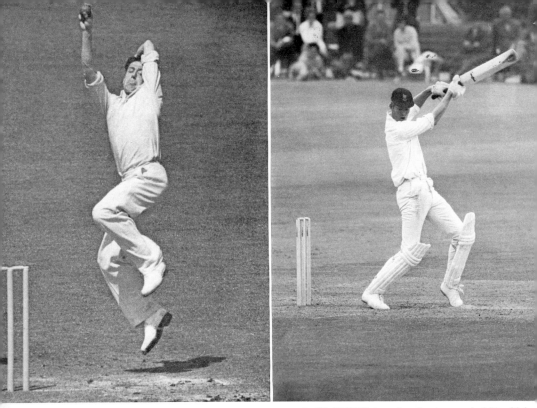

TREVOR BAILEY has been the best all-rounder of post-war years. England have found it difficult to find a well balanced side since his retirement.

A. W. GREIG has the physique and skill which might develop into a fine England all-rounder. An exciting batsman, a spectacular fielder anywhere and a bowler of possibilities. He would be a good one to fill the breach.

KEN BARRINGTON was a fighter. No one has brought more intense concentration and application to English cricket. In consequence, the enemy were always after his scalp and in this picture he is seen despatching Charlie Griffith off his eyebrows at Sabina Park, Jamaica. (*Gleaner Photo*)

M. H. DENNESS (KENT) *left*, A. JONES (GLAMORGAN) *right* AND
B. W. LUCKHURST (KENT) *below* are all mature, well tried county batsmen
who have been on the edge of higher honours for a long time. Any one of them
would wear the England cap with distinction.

UNDERWOOD AND WILSON. Derek Underwood of Kent and Don Wilson of Yorkshire, enjoying great success with their contrasting styles. Each is a wholehearted cricketer – God's gift to a captain – for both are never happier than when they are bowling. In the sixties, Wilson has been at his best on good wickets, whereas Underwood has been a killer on any wicket which offers a little help. In the seventies I can see Underwood proving his worth on the shirt fronts and Wilson wreaking more havoc on 'the turners'.

GEOFF BOYCOTT AND JOHN EDRICH. These two opening batsmen have served England well and are our best pair since Hutton and Washbrook.

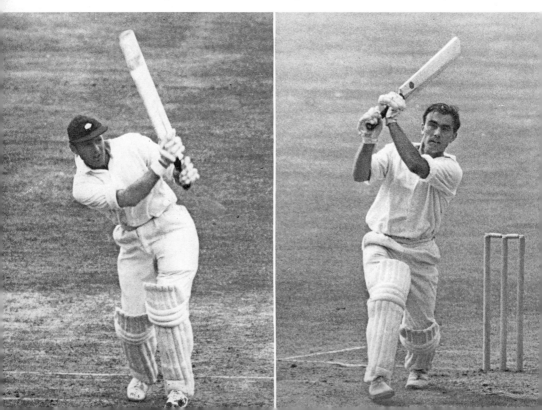

JOHN SNOW, DAVID BROWN AND ALAN WARD. For England to bring back the Ashes in 1971 we are looking to these to make the early breaks.

A MEMORY TO TREASURE. I could never take my eyes off Sir Leonard Hutton on the several occasions I was privileged to bat with him on my first tour of Australia. Here he late cuts one down very hard so that it bounces over the slips' heads. It was of major concern to me that I should not run him out and I was probably just in the throes of deciding whether a quick single to short third man was safe.

P. B. H. MAY, one of the greatest batsmen of all time. I enjoyed many partnerships with him. Here is a typical picture of him on the rampage. He gave everything he had to every stroke he played, as if each one might have cost him his life. (*Sport and General*)

TONY LOCK caught the most spectacular catches I have ever seen. Here he dives full length to catch a full blooded drive from Sobers off his own bowling in a Test match at Headingley. (*Sport and General*)

crisis, it was Trevor who moved up to number one. Typically, in that murderous series for opening batsmen in 1958-59, he made a score that stood as the highest of them all until Richardson succeeded in the last Test.

And when he moved up the order to open there was always some kind of trouble in filling his place at number six. Either a specialist batsman went in there and was left high and dry with his innings unfinished, or else an extra bowler came in and the tail was too long. In many ways Bailey was an indispensable player.

His strength really as a batsman was the bloody-mindedness that made him implacable. It was this quality too, which made him utterly unpredictable. A business man in Australia put up a £100 prize for the first batsman to hit a six, a wager which caused a book to be opened in the M.C.C. party. As I remember it, there were three non-starters in the betting — Bailey and the two left-handers, Richardson and Subba Row. There was nearly a fourth, myself, but in the end bookmaker's caution triumphed because it was remembered that somebody had occasionally seen me go wild with a hook. The winner of course, was Trevor Bailey! It was an indication of how little we knew him even after years of playing with him. He quite casually lifted the ball over the sightscreen, and then to rub it in, complained that he had not timed it.

His bowling was shrewd and incisive (except when he was bowling wide down the leg-side to prevent Australia winning the Leeds Test March of 1953!). The sheer expertise of the man can never have been displayed more than in the Kingston Test Match of the 1953-54 series. I was not present, but I have been there many times since and seen the conditions, so that I readily accept Godfrey Evans' version of the affair.

It was the last chance for England to draw a series which they had started by losing the first two matches. Hutton lost the toss to Stollmeyer and returned to the dressing room where he sat in the corner like a ghost prepared to believe that his cause was beyond hope.

In the pitch itself there was a touch of moisture, probably not enough to have been noticed in England. According to Evans only one bowler moved the ball at all, and he only a little. That was Bailey who bowled with such concentrated skill and determination that he took seven wickets for thirty-four runs. Hutton, in his relief, scored 205 and England won by nine wickets.

The logical successor to Hutton when he stood down from the captaincy in 1955, was Bailey. He had the experience, the knowledge, the hardness of character and the skill to make him acceptable both as player and leader and succession seemed natural.

He would have made a very good captain, yet predictably he found it hard to live with authority and suddenly he was gone from the reckoning. Instead the post went to Peter May, at that stage not quite ready for the responsibility of captaincy of England. A couple of years of Bailey might well have averted the tangles that affected the leadership of England even through to the '60s, and more important might have kept Peter May longer in the game.

The 1960s

The 1960s

In a decade which saw an abnormal amount of legislation, the tragedy was the premature retirement of Peter May. No side can be the same once it has lost a batsman to be rated among the best five in the world of his time, especially when it can be anticipated that he has five or six years of service still in front of him. When May, still in his early thirties, left the game the pain England suffered was two-fold for he also created a captaincy crisis that was to bring confusion for years to come.

The irony of May's spell as captain which lasted from 1955 to 1959 (give or take the occasional Test Match after that date), was that he came to the leadership too early and left it too soon. There was nobody ready to take it over once he had gone. Another couple of years of May would have enabled an acceptable successor to emerge from the ruck of contenders and so avoided the public debate that went on over the merits of Dexter, Sheppard, Mike Smith and myself.

This in itself was less important than the unseen context that went on within the game as the establishment embarked on a campaign to take away some of the power of the players. The

71

disaster in Australia in 1958-59 had shown that individual professionalism when it progressed beyond a certain point, had vices
of its own. Largely because of it a good side had splintered into a
dozen different parts.

There was also a feeling at the time that too much commercial-
isation had entered the game. Those were the boom years for
players, of advertising contracts and newspaper revelations, and the
conviction grew among the hierarchy that the power of the
professional had become too great.

In the inner circles of cricket it was not a happy time. To restore
the balance Walter Robins, an old style fire and brimstone amateur
and a one-time captain of Middlesex, was brought in to manage
the M.C.C. tour of West Indies in 1959. Understandably with two
factions in opposition, there was some strain. In the middle of it all
was Peter May, a professional-type captain of amateur status. The
pressure of the situation told on him at a time when he was still
recovering from the shocks in Australia of a year before and when
his health was in decline.

He was seriously ill before the end of the West Indies tour and
flown home for an operation. He played again for England after
that, but spasmodically and without any great enthusiasm. The
zest had withered and when eventually he decided to leave the
game for business — years before his time — his disenchantment was
plain. The decision surprised nobody who knew him, yet it was
clearly a dreadful one from the point of view of cricket. He obviously
still had so much to offer; so much that years later when he had
become a Test selector I could hear the wonder in the voice of a man
playing regularly for England who asked: "How can he sit up there
and pick men he must know are only half as good as he is now?"

The passing of May left a void at the top. A new captain was needed and, in the general reckoning I suppose I was the most likely candidate. My credentials were similar to May's and as a county captain I had established myself in the Test team. The one thing that was wrong in the context of what was required, was my own character. With the revolution going on within the game and the England side in the throes of being rebuilt, the man picked for the job, had of necessity to be a raving extrovert. I was far from that. It was quite impossible for me then or now for that matter, to make flamboyant gestures and issue rallying calls. Then it mattered. Now it does not.

I led the side a number of times of course, mainly in the absence of May, without deluding myself that I was anything like ready for permanent appointment. It was not that I was frightened of the job, or unconfident, but simply that I was not ready for it.

I have said that May received the captaincy too early, and clearly it was a struggle for him to cope with the responsibility. Yet he was better suited then than I was in the early 1960s. At least it was made a little easier for him by the fact that he led Surrey who were in the process of winning the Championship seven times. A successful county side makes for an increase of stature and confidence in the captain, whilst I was leading Kent, a side struggling fitfully in the bottom half of the table.

* * *

In 1961 I captained England in the first two Test Matches against Benaud's Australians. From the start the undertaking was purely on a caretaker basis and once May was fit he came back to take over for the last three Tests.

By 1962 the situation had become much more complicated with three men on trial as potential leaders of the M.C.C. party to Australia the following Winter. The public saw only two men in the role — Dexter and myself — although there is no doubt that David Sheppard was also strongly in the running although he did not lead England in a match in the home series against Pakistan.

Dexter led in the first two matches against Pakistan, the first of which England won by an innings and the second by nine wickets. To the everlasting bafflement, I am sure, of people who read the scores in years to come, he played under my captaincy in the Third Test Match.

In fact that is how it turned out. Under me England won by an innings at Leeds, and then Dexter came back to lead in the last two matches of the series, but by the time the fourth match was played I was even out of the reckoning as a player as I was unfit and David Sheppard opened the innings at Nottingham. He scored eighty-three. However, by then he had already become involved in another facet of the controversy that had developed around the England captaincy.

* * *

Among M.C.C. and the various bodies of selectors there is no doubt that David Sheppard was always envisaged as the man with the right qualifications to lead England. He was a good opening batsman, which was one of our weaknesses, having played in 1952 when the great England side of two years later was being formed. He was also a good enough catcher to stand close to the wicket alongside Lock, Ikin and Watkins.

When there had been one last convulsive effort to stop the move to professional captaincy under Hutton, Sheppard was the man put forward by those cherishing the amateur tradition. There is no doubt in my mind that had he been able to play cricket regularly he would have become England's captain for as long ago as 1954 he had been marked down as Hutton's deputy, having been put in charge of the side against Pakistan at Trent Bridge when Hutton was unavailable.

Sheppard's welfare work in the East End of London kept him away from county cricket for all except occasional games and so he slipped out of the international reckoning. Yet in 1962 as the hunt for May's successor grew, so his name came up again and still so impressive were his qualifications that Walter Robins, presumably after consultation with the other selectors, questioned him tentatively on the possibility of his taking the side to Australia. He was doubtful about it as his work within the Church kept him fully occupied, but after consultation with his Bishop began to think more seriously about the matter. It became a question of getting himself ready for cricket again as he was not prepared to go unless he could first prove his entitlement to a place in the party.

He played a few games for Sussex and was not happy with the result. Not only was his batting out of touch but his fielding caused him worry as well. After a long spell out of the game he found catching and moving more difficult.

Gradually his cricket improved until finally he went to Lord's to play for the Gentlemen against the Players with the name of the captain for Australia due to be announced on the second evening of the match. By then the feeling was abroad that he had only to say that he had found his touch for him to be handed the job. Among those playing the game he was by then very much the favourite. Only form stood between him and the captaincy. I tend to think that this is how Sheppard himself saw the situation.

By the time the appointment was to be announced there was no question about his form any more. In the first innings he had taken 112 off a Players' attack that included Trueman, Shackleton and Titmus.

In the short time left to him at the end of the second day he scored thirty runs of apparently the highest quality. Taken at its face value that should have been the decisive innings.

Sheppard was in the bath, the rest of the players having gone to a party in the Tavern, when a journalist put his head round the dressing room door and asked if he had any comment to make on the appointment of the captain for Australia. "It's Dexter," he said.

Such then was the confusion that followed the premature retirement of Peter May, adding as it did to the already considerable confusion that lingered on after the 1958-59 tour of Australia. It was a time of convulsions within the game.

* * *

The official ending of the division between amateurs and professionals in cricket brought mourning in some circles. It was seen as the end of a colourful era, yet my experience as a player had suggested that the distinction had ended many years before it received official recognition. Some amateurs still used separate dressing rooms from the rest of the team, and some if they had incomes of their own took no money from the game. Equally, others were still called amateurs within the meaning of the term, yet took fixed expenses from their counties. By the time the administrators got round to eliminating the distinction between the amateur and the professional, the amateur had already gone. They were simply recognising an accomplished fact.

By amateur I mean not a status judged by the narrow yardstick of money but a type of cricketer who had flair and character allied to a certain waywardness. He had almost disappeared by 1955, swept away in the tide of professionalism. For any player to exist at top level he had to adopt professional methods. Peter May was a case in point. He had all the qualifications to be accepted as an old-style amateur, yet his cricket was as dedicated as Hutton's.

The real amateur, the last of the breed, was personified by Freddie Brown, a big, colourful man who looked right in a neckerchief and a multi-coloured cap. He represented a social age that has been gone a long time now.

* * *

The occupational hazard with which cricketers live is the belief apparently held by all those not actually occupied in the business of playing, that their brand of cricket is inferior to that of their predecessors. It is a charge that seems to be levelled by each succeeding generation of cricket watcher. When I was young people even scorned the great Hutton and his partner Washbrook and spoke with animation of what Hobbs, Sutcliffe and Sandham would have done to Lindwall and Miller. Now they chide us with references to Hutton and May, and already I can sense them savouring the name of Graveney.

Nowadays the situation is even worse because there seems to be a school of thought that equates the financial problems of the game with the way it is played. The counties are losing money... how can you expect anything else the way they play the game these days? If the answer were as simple as that the financial troubles would be solved overnight by committees simply giving an ultimatum to the players to score at sixty runs an hour for the next five months or get the sack. Unfortunately other factors like full employment, the rise of other sports and the widening of social interests have affected spectator habits.

What I will not accept is that the game is in any way inferior in quality now to what it has been. Entertainment may be less, I grant that, but the best players are probably as good as ever they were, the individual skills of the bulk of the men playing the game have improved. I have to admit that today there is no English player in the class of Hobbs, Hammond or Bradman. But I am sure we have bowlers and fielders as good as ever.

I take a close interest in many sports and there is not one that I can think of in which the standard has not improved in modern times. I can see no reason why cricket should be the exception. It would seem to me to be a natural law that any sport which continues to be played on a large scale must improve technically. Clearly the game is different from the one that used to be played, and indeed I have already spoken of the changes I have noticed in it since I started playing. I have also gone at length into the reasons for the changes — the lbw law, the deterioration of pitches, the advent of the seam bowler — but these in themselves have made it necessary for players to increase their skills.

I doubt even if the rate of scoring is slower if judged on the ratio of runs and the number of balls delivered. What has happened is that the over-rate has dropped and this has taken some of the spectacle from the game. The reason is easier to find than the cure — county selection committees now consider that a battery of quicker bowlers with their time-consuming runs represent a balanced attack in modern conditions. I would certainly not stand up and say that they were wrong. There is no credit in losing matches simply for the sake of raising the over-rate by including a couple of spinners on a green wicket.

Yet when counties do manage to give their slow bowlers a fair amount of work, as when Gloucestershire and sometimes Glamorgan are going well, the rate is generally around twenty-two overs an hour, and I should think that would compare reasonably with pre-war figures.

Probably there would have been then the occasional county such as Middlesex who sometimes had three leg-spinners in Robins, Greville Stevens and Peebles, who would reach twenty-five an hour, but then it was the fashion for the slow bowlers to take charge of the attack. The fast bowlers tended towards shorter, stereotyped spells — the new ball, a few minutes before and after each break, the new ball again.

In one of my early games for Kent against Middlesex I went in at 12.5 p.m. on the first day and was out at 12.50 p.m., having scored thirty-eight. I did not face a fast bowler, all my runs having come off Sims, a leg-spinner, and Young, a slow left-hander. It would not happen today — and I regret it.

In preparing material for this book I was interested to see in an old annual an investigation into what was obviously considered a deterioration of the cricket of the time. It was based on a remark by the secretary of M.C.C. who said that there had been "a frightening drop in attendances in 1951". Freddie Brown said: "Draws have increased by forty per cent since 1948...pitches are too easy-paced...five-day Test tactics are being used in county cricket." R.H. Spooner suggested: "Return to natural wickets." George Gunn went further: "Play on matting wickets."

This is a period which has come to be seen now as the latter half of a golden era in the game, one on which we look back with delight. The pitches then were a source of comfort to the batsmen, yet there seems to have been a demand for them to be allowed to degenerate into something like those we have today. As somebody who played at both times, I find that ironic, but perhaps not nearly so ironic as the vital statistic supplied by the late Roy Webber who had worked it out that the rate of scoring in the cricket which was causing all this heart-searching had dropped by one run an hour in the period 1919-1939.

Perhaps it was another case of cricket struggling to live with its past.

* * *

In 1966 there was launched upon the cricket world the Clark Report, a full investigation into the shortcomings of modern cricket, by a committee headed by David Clark, chairman of the Kent cricket committee, and which included G.O. Allen, treasurer of M.C.C., E.R. Dexter, a former England captain, D.J. Insole, chairman of selectors, two successful county captains in W.S.

Surridge and A.B. Sellers, and a number of other players and administrators.

They conducted a comprehensive inquiry which brought to light a mass of statistics and viewpoints. In the main their suggestions were rejected by the counties although in some cases they started off trains of thought which have since brought benefits to the game.

There is no point in going through the report now which is already outdated, but there was one aspect of it which continues to be of topical interest, and that was the summary of answers to the questionnaire sent to the capped players of each county. I want to record here the answers in which the 125 players who filled in the forms were so clearly massed in a majority on one side or the other that they still have significance.

The first question was a leading one. Do you enjoy playing county cricket? Yes-115, No-seven with a suspicion that most of the seven belonged to one county whose contrary vote was the result of that odd humour that sweeps through dressing rooms on rainy afternoons when play is not possible. In short, it was a joke.

I found myself becoming reflective over this question and tried to compare the degree of my contentment with my early days as a player. Despite the difficulty of the cricket now, I came to the conclusion that in some aspects I enjoyed it more. There is a togetherness now that was often missing in those days of rivalry between individual players. I like being a part of the team work of our game. I like the happiness that comes from playing for each other.

Do you believe that county cricket produces a high standard of cricket? Yes-fifty-nine, No-sixty-six. I was with the minority and

81

I think there may have been some confusion over this question. Were they asking if we thought our cricket reached a high standard within which it was played? Or were they asking if we thought we would reach a higher standard if the conditions were better?

In the sub-questions to find the reasons for this apparent despondency, two answers took on huge significance. Ninety-seven players said the poor standard of pitches were responsible, with only ten against. And ninety-one to eighteen said that they felt they had to produce reasonable figures and averages in order to safeguard their futures as professionals.

Those two answers go to the heart of the suffering in our domestic game, just as the response to "Do you believe hard, fast, true pitches will improve the standard of play?" provides the guide to the future.

Yes-117, No-six.

* * *

The overseas players have come into the county game and have raised the standard of the cricket, thus bringing a new excitement to counties who were in the throes of depression and taking the bulk of the clubs to the edge of bankruptcy. If only the actual cricket were at stake there could be little doubt that the relaxing of the qualification rules so that counties could import top-class players from abroad has been a blessing. Nobody to my knowledge has ever argued that Sobers has done anything but good for Nottinghamshire, and almost all the other imports have made an impact on our domestic competition. Very few have been failures. Unfortunately they have made an even bigger impact on the

MAGICIANS ALL. Four great bowlers. Laker and Ramadhin (*above*), Appleyard and Gibbs (*below*). How could you choose between them? Except that they were all so different in style and approach.

'THE ENEMY'. Sheahan, Chappell and Walters.

finances of the counties than they have on their cricket. In three years they have altered the whole wage structure so that the salary bills have virtually doubled. Even treating the legendary amount that is allegedly paid to Sobers as exceptional, the money paid to overseas players seems to range between £1,500 a year and over £2,500.

Yet they were brought into a game where the first-class professionals were working for the relatively small amount of £850-£900 a year. The immediate outcome is that this figure has had to be raised. It is unrealistic to expect players who could be just as successful to be content with something like half the earnings of the man next to them. So in the 1970s the income of the capped player is going to rise to a minimum of £1,500 and this must threaten disaster to a sport, which unlike soccer where there is a huge amount of money circulating, is unable to make the adjustment and still keep twenty players on the staff.

Until now the height of ambition of most counties has been to keep ticking over. The economy has been finely balanced. Now that balance is being upset so that the traditional ways of raising revenue are no longer enough. Either there will have to be a drastic reduction in the size of playing staffs (which I would oppose) or else there will have to be more sponsorship than there has been so far with a great influx of money through football pools.

If there is still to be competition for the monied counties like Yorkshire, Warwickshire and Glamorgan from the rest of the counties, then an economic revolution is needed inside the game. It is a revolution I shall discuss later.

From a playing point of view it must be an advantage to have two good players injected into each side, and for the spectators it gives better value for money. Not least important is the hidden pleasure that comes from seeing the ease with which the overseas players fit into their county teams. In its limited way it is an object lesson in integration.

There is a drawback though. I feel that the availability of the top players to the public detracts to a certain extent from the big matches. People who can see Kanhai six days a week for five months are not filled with the same excitement at the thought of seeing him in a Test Match. The players lose some of their mystery; familiarity takes away from the drama.

* * *

It is unlikely that there has ever been a cricketer who has played under such personal pressure as Basil D'Oliveira. He has played for so much more than personal success and although he would probably not admit it there must have been a sense of mission in his efforts. Perfectly-mannered, unruffled when everybody else was becoming overheated he championed a cause against injustice. It is an insufferable burden for a man to have to carry, whose ambition is simply to play cricket.

Almost everything about D'Oliveira invites admiration. It is incredible that he should have broken through to Test cricket from a background so devoid of opportunity. To hear him talk about his cricket in Cape Town is to recognise the validity of his claim that he knew nothing about the game until he arrived in England and that he started learning it in the Lancashire League. He was apparently playing something which in its lack of sophistication was akin to village cricket in England. Yet he must have been fantastically successful at it to have had the confidence to come here and play as a professional.

He is a phlegmatic man who bats better in a crisis than at any other time. As his life has been made up mostly of crisis, I suppose that is understandable. It is as a batsman who bowls enough to be considered an all-rounder that he has made his mark in English cricket, yet I think it was as a bowler that he had his best chance of achieving greatness. Had he come to England as a youngster and been able to devote years to working at his bowling I believe he would have been a tremendous bowler — a seamer in the Tom Cartwright mould, quicker than he is now and with more variations, but basically a similar type of bowler.

As a batsman he intrigues me for technically he is the complete opposite of myself. He decides on his stroke very late and is a late hitter of the ball relying on his strength, his timing and a short backlift for power. The straight six he hit off Wes Hall at Leeds in 1966 would have been quite beyond me. I make my decision much earlier although I might still strike late, I need time to select and set myself for the stroke. To hit a fast bowler for six I would need to be gathering myself almost before the ball left his hand. D'Oliveira played his shot so late he appeared to be digging the ball out of the pitch.

It was this factor which made opening the innings harder for me in England where the ball moves late. Had I become a regular opening batsman I would have needed to refashion my technique. On the other hand my method seems better suited to conditions overseas where the ball swings less and comes on faster. It is no coincidence that my best performances have been on tour. Equally I think it is no coincidence that D'Oliveira's one failure as an England player was in West Indies. For all his success in non-white cricket in South Africa, it seems to me that his method is not so well suited to overseas cricket if there is pace in the wickets. I am not saying that he would not succeed on fast wickets were he given more chance to play on them – I am emphasising his outstanding skill on slow wickets.

For the first time in the history of Test cricket two established players were dropped from the England side and publicly admonished for slow scoring by a selection committee which had constantly reiterated their demand for positive cricket. The victims were Barrington and Boycott, two batsmen in the front rank of those to have emerged since the war.

Their punishment was a sign of the age. It is unlikely that it could have happened at any other time. Clearly, the situation would not have arisen in the 1930s when the game was more open and consequently the attitudes of players were different.

In its way it showed more clearly than any plea by a batsman who is always half suspected of trying to hide his own craven lack of initiative, the control which the bowler has taken over the game. That Barrington and Boycott, two experienced players and successful run-makers, should get into such a jam that they had to be punished is really extremely revealing.

There are certain players who because of their characters and their physical strength, their type of talent will break-through and play their own style of game whatever the conditions. There are not many of these – Pollock, Dexter, Lloyd are three who come to mind quickly. The rest of us play as well as we can within the context of the conditions. For us either Cartwright or Underwood would make life difficult and together they might make it unbearable. Everything has militated in their favour, the pitches, the defensive length, even the lacquer on the ball which is now so durable that Cartwright will still have one side of the ball shining red after seventy overs. In the old days you could not have got the shine back on the ball had you sent it to a French polisher.

In these circumstances Barrington and Boycott were dropped, perhaps not so much for what they did (or failed to do) but as a warning from the selectors to every other batsman in the country. They said in effect "we recognise the conditions for what they are, but it is up to each batsman to exercise his ingenuity to break the deadlock. It is not enough to play passively in the face of good bowling, waiting and hoping for the bad one to come along frequently enough to keep the score moving."

Through Barrington and Boycott they were reminding the players that the game is an entertainment and that they must share the responsibility for seeing that it is played entertainingly.

***

The tragedy in the life of Ken Barrington was that he never devised a way of taking his sense of humour to the crease. As a result Test cricket destroyed a little more of him with every match. He and possibly Len Hutton, who although he had even more talent was just as vulnerable to stress, will be cited for evermore as examples of the nervous strain imposed by Test cricket on its top performers.

Barrington, a sad case for he literally risked his health playing for England, appeared on the surface to have all the qualities necessary to absorb the main pressures. He had a huge sense of fun which enabled him to be an effective comic on the field and a welcome touring companion. In almost any subject outside cricket he could see the streak of humour that lightened its seriousness. But he never saw the humour in batting.

We are all nervous on Test Match mornings, but nobody suffered in the way that Ken suffered. Almost as a matter of course his health began to deteriorate as a Test Match came closer. With his career at its peak he suffered from an inability to sleep that saw him patrolling his hotel room at four in the morning. Yet when the crisis came in the Test itself, it was Barrington you wanted to see going out to meet it because you knew that he had extraordinary depths of determination.

The sheer labour of being a dedicated cricketer stretched him to the utmost. It had been like that from the start. He had gone to the Oval as a leg-break bowler and left it twenty years later having compiled batting figures that entitled him to an historic place in the game without being a truly dynamic batsman. There was no room for light relief in the effort that took him up that mountain.

The dedication of the man was apparent even in his spells of bowling in the minor matches of a tour. Not for him the light-heartedness that usually shows through when a batsman is given a few overs of exercise. He bowled properly using a full range of wrist-spin studiously learned. When he morally beat a man or had a catch dropped, he suffered.

He could not help but care. If he had his career to play again I think he might be prepared to exchange a few of his runs for the ability just to stand back from himself occasionally when batting and take a detached look around. Through no effort of my own, I have always found that my sense of humour has accompanied me to the crease, even in a Test Match. It might only amount to a wry smile at a passing remark, or perhaps nothing more than an inward surge of amusement at something I have seen and interpreted as funny even though it would have raised not a flicker with anybody else. Whatever it is, it is not going to amount to much because Test Matches are not hilarious places, but it is enough to lift the inward tension. It is an invaluable safety valve.

Unfortunately for Ken Barrington there was no such outlet.

* * *

Ted Dexter was playing a round of golf in Adelaide in company with Norman Von Nida and Gary Sobers and displaying such unbridled power that Von Nida said of him: "He is the best natural striker to come out of England since Henry Cotton." The same parallel can be applied to his batting on his "on days". He is an alarming hitter of the ball whose brilliance raises interesting questions of its own. Was Wally Hammond as good as this? Were Fry, Maclaren and those other men whose names have been reverently handed down to us, like this?

When he played at the top of his form he played incomparable cricket. There is no need to dig into the memory to recall his batting, for his innings push their way through all the other memories I have.

Brisbane 1962...seventy runs in a first innings that was all aggression; ninety-nine in the second in two and three quarter hours. Barbados 1959, the First Test Match in a series in which the fast bowlers repeatedly examined every man's courage...Dexter 136 not out. Lord's 1963...Dexter a pulverising seventy that included dismissive treatment of Griffith, a bowler whose action made it hard to pick up the line of the ball.

When he was going like this he was surely in a class of his own. These were innings of cricket perfection, of infallible technique, of immense strength, of extraordinary skill and perfect temperament.

It is sad that Dexter has not stayed in the game as a regular player. It is entirely his business that he has not and it is none of mine to question his actions. He is a man of instant ambition and wide-ranging interests and he has occupied himself with journalism, golf, flying and countless other things. There are those who will argue that the Dexter way is right and that a man wins no accolades for spending the best twenty years of his life hitting a ball around a field.

Take which part you will. I only know that in Dexter's spasmodic career there has been a waste of a vast cricketing talent.

* * *

Immense is the only word with which to describe the loss to England's cricket of Colin Milburn. He was eliminated at a time when he had worked out a formula for batting success and had thus assured himself a place in the Test team — probably not as an opening batsman — for years to come. The best was still ahead of him.

For most of his short career in the England team he had been unlucky in that his main batting companions had been Barrington and Boycott, both of whom were self-disciplined and preferred to play the bowling strictly on merit. This creates a difficult situation for the aggressive player who wants to pick the game up and kick it about. Graeme Pollock could do it in these circumstances. Milburn, until near the time of his accident, was not quite good enough. This blitzkrieg type of game is a very difficult one to play at Test level and he had just about come to terms with it. Where he had been too explosive, too impetuous, he had started to discipline his talents and run innings his way rather than survive on a ball to ball basis. The need for this became clear to him, I think, after a miserable tour of West Indies on which, incidentally, he revealed the princely side of his character by remaining in tremendous spirits despite his failures.

After that he used his time playing for Western Australia in the Sheffield Shield to reshape his play, and in his last innings for England before his car accident, he arrived in Pakistan to score a century that emphasised that he had got the balance right.

England would have had many brilliant innings from him over the next five years, and despite the criticisms of his fielding he was a superb catcher with lightning reactions. As he got older so he would have learned to field at slip. In success, in failure, now in adversity Milburn has shown himself to be a sterling character.

Enough to say that like Bob Barber, who had less skill, he was the type of player who dealt in streaks of success rather than consistency. Had he played his cricket in the 1930s he would have become a legend.

* * *

A strange feature of England's cricket has been the number of wicket-keepers who have been drafted into the team only to fall out again without making a real mark. Evans, that superb artist, was a constant factor in selections of his day with Griffith, McIntyre, Spooner and Brennan walking in his shadow.

But the ten years after Evans produced a complete confusion of players. There were Andrew, Brian Taylor, Swetman, and in the last Test in West Indies in 1960 because Peter May wanted his batting, Jim Parks, who scored a hundred. The nearest thing to a constant came in Murray with Millman as his number two, but Murray had no sooner seemed established than Alan Smith had pushed his way in and then Parks claimed the regular place. Now Knott has arrived and the permutating has stopped.

Australia in that time went quietly about the job of handing the wicket-keeping position down through a line of succession that took in Tallon, Langley, Grout and Jarman and covered twenty years. There was nothing feverish about their selections. They went for their man and they stayed with him.

The uncertainty started to show through in the English selections as soon as Evans finished.

That action was precipitate. He was left out of the M.C.C. party for West Indies in 1959-60 while he was still the best wicket-keeper in England and before there was anybody ready to take over from him. The choice was never indisputable again until Knott was picked

The disappointment in between was John Murray's failure to establish himself. In 1961 he kept wicket in all five Tests against Australia with tremendous polish and confidence so that his future looked secure, but in a little over a year he was out of the side. He would have seemed the best candidate of them all for with his wicket-keeping he was a decent batsman. But for injury he could almost have been in the hot spot today — making Alan Knott wait, for I maintain that he was every bit as good a player as Jarman of Australia.

Parks was the surprise of the selections. He played around fifty times for England, mainly in the taxing role of wicket-keeper and it says everything for his ability that he was able to adapt himself for such a long period. Probably a number of players have made the transition from cover-point to wicket-keeper, as Parks did, but the real achievement was in doing the job so long and so well that he came to accept himself as the side's first choice wicket-keeper. He first took over the gloves with some doubt and reluctance. Long before the end he found he was being irked by the occasional days spent in the field in second-class matches of a tour while the party's number two wicket-keeper was given a run.

The trouble was, of course, that selection of the side was influenced by the lack of an all-rounder in the batsman-bowler category. To make up the deficit the wicket-keeper had to bat and that virtually narrowed the field to a straight choice between Murray and Parks, with Parks initially getting the vote because of the runs he made. The selectors were lucky in that he developed into a competent wicket-keeper.

* * *

While wicket-keepers were lining up for admission to the Test team and young bowlers have evolved recently in encouragingly large numbers, I find myself looking anxiously for new, if not young, batsmen. Had circumstances been better than they were in 1969 and retirement and injury not struck so hard, the best five batsmen in the country would have been Boycott, Edrich, Graveney,

Barrington, and may I say it, myself. Graveney, Barrington and myself started our cricket in the early 1950s, Edrich in 1958 and Boycott in 1962. Providing merit were the only requirement and there were not some tactical exigency to be considered, all five of us would have been in the England team.

I am disappointed and a little surprised that Fletcher or Amiss, both of whom are now nearer thirty than twenty, has not pushed out one of the older ones before. The only significant batting change in the years immediately before the start of the 1970 season involved the recalling of a thirty-nine year old man, Graveney.

Because of the pitches, the amount of one-day cricket, and various other factors, batsmen now are maturing later. Because of this the whole cycle of producing Test cricketers is likely to be delayed. If batsmen now are not going to be ready for an England place until they are near thirty where once the age was twenty, then clearly the amount of time they will spend at the top is going to be shortened. Hutton, Compton, myself, to take but three examples, spent the best part of twenty years in the England team. A player coming in at thirty as a regular player will have no more than five or six years in front of him. As a result the England team will be faced with a crisis every few years of a similar type to the present one when not enough players have developed to take over the batting places.

It is a disturbing situation, and I leave you with the thought that if the game is so difficult now that Boycott and Barrington, two of the best players in the land were made to struggle sufficiently to be punished, what chance have the others got? Might there be another Compton, breaking-through at eighteen? I don't know...

* * *

The strangest player I ever saw in top-class cricket was undoubtedly Bob Barber. He defied what I like to think is the logic of the game and that is bound to leave any student of it somewhat mystified.

When with Lancashire, he was arguably the biggest bore post-war cricket has seen. If this sounds a harsh judgement I can only say that he played strokes at a frequency which made Trevor Bailey appear a hustler, yet from being a champion blocker, he moved to Warwickshire to emerge full of pugnacity and violence...a left-handed Milburn. What is more, he was prepared to produce this new found audacity in the tension of Test Matches with the result that at Sydney on Mike Smith's tour, he committed a brutal assault on the Australian attack and thus put England in a position to win the match from the first afternoon.

Two things puzzle me about Barber. I am curious to know how good he could have been, for he drifted out of Test cricket before we could see how far he was going to develop. The other thing is that if a man's cricket is an extension of his personality and character, what happened inside Barber in 1963 to enable him to play the game with a completely different approach? Did he undergo a character change?

* * *

In any cricket conversation of any length the question is almost certain to be put to me of what it was like to have Fred Trueman in the side and what was the secret of handling him. The answer is always a let down. Once you accept, as I do, that all fast bowlers are liable to be a bit more temperamental than other players and that in most cases that is why they became fast bowlers, then Trueman does not appear as exceptional. More than any other member of the team, one has to be prepared to make allowances for the fast bowler.

As far as I can recall offhand, I have played with only three who because of the equanimity of their natures did not have to have special treatment. They were Lindwall, Statham and McKenzie.

Without trying to compose a comprehensive list it comes to mind equally easily that Davidson, Miller, Heine, Loxton, Hall, Griffith, Tyson and Trueman all at times needed diplomatic handling by their captains. Any captain who is going to retain his post for any length of time recognises this and accordingly gives them individual consideration on a scale unknown by the other members of the side.

This is another aspect in which I believe the game has changed over the decades. I have spoken to old fast bowlers whose relationship to the captain seems to have been roughly on a par with that of the private and the regimental sergeant major. He bowled when ordered, at the end that was ordered, and sometimes even on a line directed by the captain. Otherwise conversation between the two was minimal.

The approach now is rather broader and altogether more human. As far as I myself am concerned – and it applies to most captains now – I have four or five bowlers who between them I have to use to the advantage as a team. This advantage I create through consultation with them picking up what information I can and recognising that as a batsman I know less about the business of bowling people out than they do. A bowler-captain, I imagine, might be more dogmatic as he will have to play an active part in the attack.

In the main I am reliant on them and except in times of crisis when a sharp decision may be needed, I prefer to run the side on a consultative basis. This in no way detracts from my position. In the end I have to take both the decision and the responsibility of things going awry.

But at least by this method I reduce the chances of having a prima donna of a fast bowler in the side who has to be chatted up constantly to keep him happy.

At times, of course, Freddie Trueman has proved to be the most controversial character in cricket. You could not be negative about him. He was a personality who demanded your attention and I found people either loved him or shied away. For my money, he was worth his weight in gold, at his best if there was hard work to be done and he could be in the centre of it.

P. J. SHARPE (YORKSHIRE AND ENGLAND) is the safest fielder I have seen and must surely be rated in the Wally Hammond class. In this picture the West Indies opening batsman, Carew, slashes hard at D'Oliveira and gets a top edge. Sharpe has anticipated brilliantly and brings off the most difficult catch a right handed slip fielder can have – at full stretch on the left hand side. He shows wonderful reflex action to get two hands to this one.

BENAUD c. COWDREY b. TRUEMAN first ball at Melbourne 1963. I think this is the catch which gave me most satisfaction. (*The Sun*)

A KENT MONOPOLY in the Test match at the Oval. Underwood claims a vital wicket which set us on the road to victory against the Australians in 1968 at the Oval. Cowdrey's and Knott's vigorous appeal in support of their Kent colleague is acceded to by another friend and Kent colleague, Umpire Arthur Fagg – now one of the great umpires of the day. (Happily there is no doubt about Redpath's dismissal).

BARRY RICHARDS (Hampshire) has taken the cricket world by storm. His performances in South Africa were reminiscent of C. J. Barnett (Gloucestershire and England) and somehow we tended to think that method and approach was not going to reappear in Test cricket.

1970 and the Future

1970 and the Future

The march forward has got to be more carefully planned than anything that has happened in the past. Until the last few years cricket has had the time and the space to develop leisurely – the County Championship is basically much the same as it was forty years ago. Now there is less space, less time. Soccer has moved in so that it has taken over most of the months of the year, and soon I do not doubt, will take over them all. There is competition from other sports and social activities on a scale never hitherto known such as golf and sailing; these were sports that offered only minor competition before. There is a sense of impatience among the public who are no longer prepared to be tolerant but who agitate to be entertained.

In this atmosphere we search for a formula which will ensure the future of cricket, a classical game born and nurtured in a time of less pressure and frenzy. Providing we find the correct formula there is a fine future for it, of that I am convinced. We must be careful not to make the sudden dive after quick and opportunistic solutions which passes for planning among some of the game's administrators.

The first requirement is to get the balance right. I am appalled at the constant demands for programmes which virtually eliminate the three-day match and substitute instead great lumpy helpings of one-day cricket leavened only with Test Matches. Whatever joys that might bring to future summers it would have no connection with the game I have played for twenty years. A balance must be struck between the three types of cricket we now play in England — Test cricket, county cricket and one-day cricket — with the object of keeping the playing standards at the highest possible level. To achieve this, each type of cricket will have to move a little from its set course.

Test cricket may well have to make a move towards limiting overs on the first innings. In view of the scorn of county cricketers when the first innings of Championship matches were limited to sixty-five overs, we would have to think in terms of a figure which would allow the games to be played as reasonable contests.

I would suggest 120 overs which would mean scores of 300 or more on the first innings and would keep the inherent falseness of the situation down to a minimum. It would I feel make for a generally livelier approach to the game. With each side facing a second innings the matches would be thrown open earlier and the finishes would be more exciting.

Over the years the influence of the coin on Test cricket has disenchanted me more than any other single factor. I cannot believe it makes for good entertainment that one captain, by the sheer blind luck of calling right, should be allowed the opportunity to settle at the crease for two days while he builds an impregnable total. When he has finished, the public are then presented with the equally stultifying sight of the other side batting to avoid defeat in a match which they have no chance of winning, or else being bowled out on a pitch which has fallen to pieces, so robbing the match of any semblance of fairness. The toss has decided too many Test Matches for my liking. A limitation of its effect would do no harm, especially in overseas matches where it is common for the side winning the toss to bat for 200 six ball overs or more.

In many ways the future organisation of county cricket is the most important of them all, if only because it seems to be the one that attracts the bizarre theories of the apostles of change. In this section it is not the game itself which needs to be altered — that must remain as it is in essence — but the presentation of it which requires rethinking. By that I do not mean a reduction of the county game to sixteen matches a season as some counties have suggested. I can think of no quicker way to bring about the death of the game than to offer that vast army of members who keep it going, only eight home games, two of which are almost certain to be ruined by rain.

The county game is the one that has got to be handled most carefully because it is the section that creates the standards for all cricket. Men reach Test cricket and play well for England because of the skill and experience they have gathered in county cricket. The geared-up cricket which batsmen produce in the one-day encounters is a legacy of a thorough grounding in the county game.

I will support this contention as there is clearly a strong lobby ready to abandon the three-day match (I have even heard talk of one-day Test Matches!). There are two points that need to be made.

Firstly, there is no country in the world that plays Test Matches on a ration of one-day cricket. It would simply not be possible to have a Test team if one-day cricket were all. Indeed recent experience has shown that without a continuous background of cricket even such a magnificent player as Dexter has found it difficult to cross the bridge back into Test cricket again. Yet he had played regular Sunday cricket with the Cavaliers as well as the occasional warming-up match with Sussex.

Secondly, there is the more arguable point that Players' League and Gillette Cup cricket benefit from experience gained with the counties. I have frequently heard it claimed that club cricketers with their Saturday afternoon belligerence, could make just as good a fist of these competitions, an argument confounded by the fact that Minor Counties seldom get anywhere near worrying even the weakest of the first class sides when they get through to the competition.

County cricket to me then, is the key section in any development of the game. For years I have heard it claimed that whatever the current malady with cricket the cause was always the common one that we play too much cricket. A seven days a week programme is too much of course, but I would not like the Championship reduced so as to give us less. I have known days in recent seasons when in mid-season we have been in our gardens under a blazing sun wondering why on earth it was that we were not playing cricket and what was the logic of fixture-making that gave us a break at an inopportune time.

The county cricket programme does not take the zest out of English players. Indeed the opposite is the case for by its constant challenge to our skill it ensures that we have a larger reservoir of talented players than any other country.

Nor does it physically and mentally tire us. Not in a way that is recognisable until the season is over, at least. I have never failed to enjoy county cricket and I have never felt that I did not want to play it. As far as I am concerned, twenty-four matches, the present length of the Championship is the right one.

We have got to have solid cricket through the summer in our own interests, in the interests of our members, and in the interests of the huge public who follow the game through Press and television. Once we deprive them of a full programme to follow, then we really can start to mourn for the game because once their attention has wandered elsewhere, it will never come back again.

Those then, are the reasons I feel that county cricket must be kept going in its present form even though it means it being subsidised by those sections of the game that attract bigger crowds. It is too important to be judged by income alone.

Once the size of the crowds comes into the reckoning, then clearly the week-ends become a problem as they are the only two days on which the majority of people are free to attend. I can see that a league match with its limited course and result suits their palate admirably, but I am less taken with the thought of the league programme taking up all the available Sundays in the summer.

The best watching day in the week should be available for the best cricket (i.e. county cricket) on at least some occasions in the summer. To make this possible I see no reason why the season should not be extended to last from the last week in April until the end of September. I know the problems of Autumn weather, of fading light, of the ball made slippery by the dew, but they cause me less fear than the plans to skimp the season at the expense of county cricket. Weather in England is variable at any time of the year, yet we have had to learn to play through. The ideal in a longer season would be for a club to play three games at home then three games away so that local interest could be sustained over a period rather than splintered or lost altogether when a match is rained off.

But whatever happens there must be no potted championship. I am sure I speak too, for all those treasurers who depend on the income that comes annually from 7,000 or so members and enables the clubs to keep going.

* * *

The answer to the financial problems of County Championship cricket must now lie in sponsorship. Backing by industrial companies has already been seen to work within the game where Players' and Gillette have taken up the one-day cricket, and it has become a considerable factor in golf and tennis and practically every professional sport. I see no reason why sponsorship should not be just as effective in three-day cricket.

I would suggest for investigation a system by which the sponsors of all three cricket competitions — the county game and the two one-day competitions — contribute sums of money to a pool from which would come the players' wages. As all types of cricket benefit from the skills gained in county cricket it is only fair that they should all help with its finance.

The wages of the playing staff represent the bigger outgoings in a county's finances and without them there would be less of this demoralising talk of financial ruin. The counties' own takings would then be available for ground upkeep and improvements, with more attention being paid to the needs of the public than is now possible.

106

In any case, the time has come when there will have to be a rethinking of the paying of players. The present system is unsuited to the situation that is developing within the game now that overseas players have rasied the wage level and that some counties have so much more money to spend than others.

There are two stipulations necessary in any new scheme — the wages must be good to make it worthwhile for the best talent to stay in the game, and they must be controlled to prevent the slide towards a transfer market which is already coming dangerously close. Since the relaxation of the qualification rules it has become relatively easy for a player to change counties.

A common wage scale throughout the counties with an adjusting mechanism so that the best players receive the most, would certainly be fairer than the free-for-all which is causing so much unrest at the moment. At the root of most of the labour troubles in a modern society is the amount of money a man takes home in his pocket. Cricket, where the length of service is comparatively short, is no exception.

The money from the sponsorship pool could probably be used through a committee consisting of elected representatives of the players and members of the Test and County Cricket Board. As this would be a matter concerning only domestic cricket, there would be no need for M.C.C. to become involved.

The concern of the committee would be to see that the individual players had reasonable incomes and that the counties were able to run big enough playing staffs to ensure that the standard of the game is maintained. I can see the financial reasoning behind the Essex decision to cut their staff to thirteen — and in fact this made it possible for them to make a profit in 1969 — but it is not

107

a trend I appreciate. It needs only one player to be called into the Test team and another to fall ill and the team is playing at a level which is unfair to itself, the other sixteen counties in the Championship and the members. I would not like these small staffs to become accepted as normal.

From the pool too, I believe the umpires and the head groundsmen of each county should be paid. The importance of the umpires is obvious, and the constant talk about better pitches means nothing if the best groundsmen cannot be attracted into first class cricket. It sickens me that counties with their desperate need for good wickets should lose their groundsmen to a bank or works sports ground in the vicinity who are offering an extra five pounds a week and a rent-free house. The best cricket must have the best groundsmen, else it will not stay best for long.

Obviously a sponsorship scheme such as I have suggested would need thorough investigation and planning. I think it is urgent to find some way of making the counties viable so that they can avoid the constant compulsion to look back over their shoulders.

* * *

From a playing point of view I have high hopes that batsmen will be liberated by the new lbw law which was introduced for the 1970 season. I trust now that the good batsmen will be able to get on the back foot and produce that range of off-side shots that have, of necessity, been limited in recent years.

Hobbs, Bradman, Hammond and the rest made their initial batting movement on to the back foot even though they finally came forward. They were in a pushing-off position with the back foot acting as a spring so that they could move forward quickly if necessary. It is something I have found myself doing on overseas wickets, but seldom in England. Significantly I consider that my best batting has been played overseas. Now, in their efforts to eliminate pad play, the authorities have taken the lbw law back closer to what it was before 1935. There are still going to be those days of grey skies low over the ground with the ball swinging alarmingly when forward defensive play will provide the best means of survival. But on the other days when the sun is shining and the pitch is dry, I hope to see the back foot strokes on display again.

A number of seasons will be needed before it is clear how much of an effect the change in the lbw law has had. One is not enough. For many batsmen in the game it will mean a widening of their method on a scale they have not known before and to achieve that they will need to rid themselves of some of the suspicion that has become an essential quality in their play. They will need time.

* * *

The outstanding ambition left to me is easier to define than to execute. I would like, in this Winter of 1970-71 to be a member of the side which beats Australia on their own grounds and bring back the Ashes. I started too well in the business of Test cricket serving under Sir Leonard Hutton in a team which saw victory over the Australians at Sydney, Melbourne and Adelaide. Only Tom Graveney and I of that team are still playing, and so comprehensive was England's victory that it would never have occurred to me then that in sixteen years' time with retirement looming closer, I would still be looking for my second victory in Australia.

But I am, and the need for it has become stronger over the

years. For an English cricketer there is still something special about playing Australia even though they currently rate some distance behind South Africa and have not been as devastating as West Indies in the 1960s. In our relationship is a mixture of tradition and sentiment. The sight of the green cap of our oldest enemy does something to me.

I am far from convinced that in the six series since 1956 when England plus Laker beat them, that they have been the better side. Yet they have been the successful side. Perhaps this indicates that on their part too, they have a special feeling about playing against England. They are certainly our most unrelenting opponents for even in those occasional series when their team lacks its usual quality, they seem to find extra reserves of doggedness and determination.

It is because of that that I see no long-term demise resulting from their shattering experience in South Africa. They are a resilient, competitive bunch who will be waiting for us just as confidently as ever. It is quite on the cards that they will react even more fiercely after the hurts they suffered in South Africa. The memory of the way they handled us in 1958-59 after their drubbing in England two years before will stay with me for ever.

The English preparation for this campaign has been less ordered than it should have been. When I took the side to West Indies in 1967 I saw that as the start of a period which would culminate in this Winter's meeting with Australia. Basically we had a new side with only Barrington, Graveney and myself in the mature class. With an attack that was both young and highly efficient we had the chance to fashion a team which with ambition centred on Australia, would attain its peak about now.

The drawback was that the programme which was going to bring us to this eminence fell apart. We started the right way by winning in West Indies and when we came back, there was a tremendous confidence in the side. Australia were in England that Summer and a real fight of a series was in prospect. Instead it rained...and rained...and rained and the sides could hardly get to grips at the times when it mattered most. Nor was the following Winter any better because the tour of South Africa which might have been a classic encounter between the two best teams in the world at that time, was cancelled and a short trip to Pakistan substituted. This became largely meaningless from a cricket point of view because of the time spent dodging rioters. Since then, of course, the South African tour of England has also been cancelled.

For one reason and another 1969 found England deprived of Barrington, Milburn, Graveney and myself. All credit to Ray Illingworth that without four leading batsmen he was able to take us to victory over West Indies and New Zealand. This provided wonderful opportunities out of the blue for Sharpe, Hampshire, Fletcher and Denness. It was good to see Alan Ward of Derbyshire making such an impressive debut, for remembering Frank Tyson, he more than anyone else could wrest back the Ashes in Australia. There was no Winter tour last year, although M.C.C. took a few of England possibles to the Far East. Here Geoff Boycott was able to experiment with his new contact lenses and made a lot of runs, much to the relief of his admirers.

For my part I had the luck to be invited to captain the Cavaliers Team to Jamaica in January for three weeks and then after a short break at home to lead the Duke of Norfolk's team in Barbados, Trinidad and the Windward Islands.

The seasons are changing, sadly, and in Jamaica we were badly hit by rain. Nevertheless, there was a lot of good cricket played by my very strong side, a blend of youth and experience — Cowdrey, Sobers, Dexter, Evans, Trueman and Murray alongside Sharpe, Luckhurst, Ward, Underwood and Snow. Jamaica cricket has been in the doldrums, but now they are on the way up again and it was pleasing to feel that our short visit has made a worthwhile contribution.

The Duke of Norfolk, and I do not know a keener cricketer, decided in the Autumn that he would like to take the twelve best young cricketers in England to the Caribbean for a month. He felt that this could be of great assistance to the selection committee at home, provide invaluable experience for several of the Australian possibles, and he in his turn sought only the reward of watching them enjoy their cricket and the fun of following the fortunes of those who are good enough to be picked for Australia. Alan Ward, for instance, was given the practical taste of how hard it is to bowl overseas and so too was Derek Underwood. Denness, Sharpe, Greig, Birkenshaw and Griffith were all given an unique experience whilst I, too, was greatly helped by getting going again in the sunshine after such a long lay off with my ruptured achilles tendon. In fact, I am absolutely certain that I would not have been fully fit for the 1970 English season without those two trips.

Incidentally, these two trips highlight cricket's debt to sponsors. Whereas His Grace was very generous himself, I know he was grateful for the backing of his team by Gillette and that the tour of Jamaica would not have taken place but for the help of Rothmans. These have always been two good friends of cricket.

I am hopeful that our young team will do well in Australia. I am a little sad, too, that the organised build-up that we had planned after the successful West Indies trip of 1968 could never materialise. It has been no fault of the players, nor the selectors, that each series has seemed to start again. If the team spirit can be forged in the early weeks, we shall be half way to victory.

It is important this time that England should bat well in Australia. It sounds an obvious enough requirement, yet I say it because it has been my impression of my tours there that England have not generally batted up to their capabilities. Even the indisputable victories of 1954-55 were largely based on totals that would have looked fairly shabby had we not possessed an attack of such quality. The most runs in the series were scored by Peter May, yet he averaged only thirty-nine.

Too often we seem to have gone to Australia wondering how we were going to bowl them out, only to find that it is our batting that lets us down. We seem to take so long to adapt. The last six weeks invariably bring all-round batting performances of a sort we have not known in the first half of the tour. Quite often I have felt that we were all striking our best just as we were about to leave for home. In contrast England have a dreadful record at Brisbane, the city which stages the First Test. This time, with a younger and less experienced party than usual, a quicker settling-in period is essential.

* * *

Statistics tell me that the faster bowlers have been the most effective Englishmen in Australia. A table from 1932, which seems far enough back to make a point, taking in the best bowlers from medium-pace upwards, looks like this:—

1932-33: Larwood, Voce, Hammond and Allen...78 wickets in the series.

1936-37: Voce, Farnes, Hammond, Allen...66 wickets.

1946-47: Bedser, Yardley, Edrich...35 wickets.

1950-51: Bailey, Bedser, Brown...62 wickets.

1954-55: Tyson, Statham, Bailey...56 wickets.

1958-59: Trueman, Statham, Tyson, Loader, Bailey...35 wickets.

1962-63: Trueman, Dexter, Statham...44 wickets.

1965-66: Jones, Brown, Knight...34 wickets.

There were two exceptional series in that list when spinners were the most effective individual bowlers — 1958 when Laker took fifteen wickets, and 1946 when Wright had twenty-three.

This then, is the argument of statistics. Reason tells me to keep an open mind. My own experience indicates that Australian pitches are changing, that they are not the same flat, fast, everlasting strips of clay that they used to be. Sydney, for instance, can vary from being a seam bowlers' dream of home to a slow turner. Like wickets the world over, those in Australia have lost some of their pace, an argument supported by the statistics I have quoted from which it is clear that the fast bowlers have been less effective of late.

Whatever the conditions now, the variety of the England attack ensures that it will always be effective. The job of the captain is to get together the keenest combination, the one most eager to make the challenge. On tour that means far more than any preconceived plan of campaign.

* * *

I look forward to seeing Walters and Sheehan bat with more than usual curiosity. I want to see how far they have improved since last we met. Both rather burst on the scene in the manner of Norman O'Neill, and both got into a tangle in England. Walters in addition had a spell of Army service to get out of his cricketing system and he may still have been suffering from the hangover from this in South Africa.

Walters, I think, is going to be very good. From the moment he came to the crease against England at Brisbane in 1965, his talent was obvious. He is a magnificent catcher and a fine athlete with it.

Ian Chappell emerged as that rare kind of Australian who looked a better batsman in England than he did on his own wickets. Despite the rain of 1968 he scored more runs than anyone else in the side, gripping the bat with the right hand in the English manner as if he had been playing county cricket all his life.

Meeting McKenzie again will be interesting, too. It is unbelievable that he could have played for Leicestershire in 1969 when pitches were favouring bowlers and taken only seventy-seven wickets.

I would have backed him for a minimum of a hundred wickets. Since then he has been dropped in South Africa, where he took only one wicket in the series at a cost of 333 runs! But I will believe in his permanent decline only when I see it. He is a bowler who generates his pace from physical strength and fitness which means that once he has got the mechanism of his body working right again he could well be just as dangerous. He is too young to write off.

* * *

* * *

The recent demise of Australia at the hands of South Africa has really depressed their current market value. Several people, each with good cricket minds, have said to me recently "You are not going to have much trouble against the Australians this Winter. It is rather disappointing they are not a bit better."

I have given each one of them a withering look. I have been four times to Australia and found victory in any match as difficult to come by as coming away from Yorkshire on the winning side! Furthermore, they are at present smarting under their wounds and they are great fighters — no one more so than Bill Lawry. I shall be surprised if he has not got a good few hours more of testing an Englishman's patience, and a very fine player he is too.

The bulk of the runs will be coming from the heart of the enemy, Ian Chappell, Doug Walters and Paul Sheehan — a formidable trio. Somehow, they could not find consistency in South Africa, but they are all too good to be below their best for long.

I think Chappell will be the biggest run scorer of the three. Extremely fit, a strong right hand, a penchant for the on side and always hungry for runs, he is no mean bowler too and a fine close fielder.

Doug Walters is a superb athlete and has a flair for batsmanship. I find his occasional lapses completely inexplicable.

From the moment I first saw Paul Sheehan playing for Sir Robert Menzies XI at Canberra, I sensed that I was watching a player of class. His long range of flowing strokes makes him a delight to watch and as his defence tightens so he will become progressively more successful. He must be a candidate for the title of best outfielder in the world today.

116

There have been several other exciting successes in the latter half of the '60s, all of whom we shall be following in the '70s.

Before I refer to the home cricketers, let me look overseas. Graeme Pollock must take pride of place and is becoming the star attraction in world cricket. It is something of a tragedy that Pollock cannot be seen in West Indies and Sobers in South Africa, for they have so much in common and I would not like to have to decide which was the better batsman. Sobers I would accord the greater player capable of the more extraordinary feats. Pollock would be the more solid and dependable. Both are immensely strong and have to be got out early.

I am sure that Mike Procter would concede that his spell with Gloucestershire has proved to be a very good finishing school. He is a very gifted cricketer and has improved dramatically these last two years. He is now a very fast bowler at times and his strange action presents an awkward proposition to the batsman. I hope for his sake that he will not be overbowled. With these overseas players coming backwards and forwards, winter and summer, the fast bowlers are going to have the biggest load.

Pakistan are developing a fine Test side. I felt terribly sad for their cricket public when our tour fell into such disarray at the hands of the political demonstrators in 1969. The Pakistan folk are cricket-crazy, and out of limited facilities a host of young talent has sprung. If I was the cricket dictator of Pakistan I would give a special award to the best four fast bowlers but they have got to be genuinely quick. The day that Pakistan can produce two fast bowlers of genuine Test Match standard, then they will be be able to take on and beat anybody.

I cannot think of four more exciting cricketers than Mushtaq (Northamptonshire) Majid (Glamorgan) Asif (Kent) and Younis (Surrey). Each one of them has really made his mark in English cricket and has captured our public's imagination. They in their turn, like Procter, have learnt more than they could possibly have imagined. Pakistan cricket should have benefited from this.

India too, can be very proud of the Lancashire wicket-keeper Engineer, an exciting, attacking cricketer. Lancashire's fortunes are on the upgrade again and Engineer has contributed very largely to this.

The overall general standard of New Zealand cricket has improved in my opinion, although they are short of some big names. The skill of Headley Howarth with his left-arm slow bowling has impressed us all. When you think how little experience he has had, it is quite remarkable that he was able to hold down all our best players in the way he did in 1969. One feels that he is going to need to get more competitive cricket so as to maintain that standard. He is one of the best slow bowlers who have come into the game for years and at a time when slow bowlers are few and far between and their lot most unenviable. It will be fascinating to see how long he can stay the course.

Of the West Indians, Sobers' contribution to Nottinghamshire has been prolific, although playing so much over these last two years has drained him physically and mentally. I think we should learn from this, and the various cricket authorities should be prepared to apply the brake upon their leading players whenever they think fit.

Lancashire have a superb batsman in Clive Lloyd, and surely now that Bland has retired, the most exciting fielder in the world. Lloyd has the richest gifts that you could imagine and as he settles to English conditions I am sure he is going to put up some remarkable scoring performances against the clock.

The same applies to Boyce of Essex, a match-winner if ever there was one. He and John Shepherd of Kent should be members of West Indian cricket for years to come. If Shepherd can keep clear of back injury, he will be an automatic all-rounder in any Test team.

I have a vivid recollection of the match Godfrey Evans played at Lord's in 1959. He made one or two mistakes but otherwise was keeping wicket better than anyone else in England. The time had come, the Selectors felt, when they must be looking ahead for the next England wicket-keeper and so Godfrey Evans was retired to the wings, perhaps before his time. I remember watching him very closely in the later matches when he was still in top form, trying to catch the Selectors' eyes again. I wondered "Will we ever see his like again?" He had been a fine boxer and this had helped him. He took the most awful knocks but they never seemed to affect him. He was always cheerful, optimistic and gay. It was always fun to play with or against him, and like all the "greats" he was capable of rising to the occasion when it really mattered.

What a coincidence that within a year or two of his retirement a little seventeen year old was sent along by the Second XI captain to play for Kent in a friendly match at Folkestone against Cambridge University. I had never met him before although I had heard of his promise. I well recall seeing him in the third over of the match diving full length to his left and clinging on to a half chance.

I did not say anything but as he picked himself up off the floor, beaming all over his face, I knew instinctively that we had found a wicket keeper in the Evans mould. If anyone is ever going to be as good as Godfrey Evans, it might just be Alan Knott. He still has some way to go and yet he has such gifts that it is all within his grasp. What is more, he will probably be a very fine batsman and, just as important, he is a sterling character who wears the England cap proudly.

There are two left-handers I would like to talk about. Early in the Sixties there appeared on the scene another Edrich, a left-handed batsman who was getting a reputation for being very suspect, flashing away outside the off stump. There also appeared in Kent a peculiar type slow left arm bowler who for some apparently inexplicable reason kept getting wickets. His name is Derek Underwood.

The pundits, as usual had a lot to say about them both. "John Edrich — yes, very strong, good eye, good temperament too, but rather a pity that he will get sorted out in the big stuff. Shame; he could have made a player."

And again, the pundits: "Derek Underwood — Nice boy — good trier — will bowl all day. Pity he does not do enough with it. In a year or two he will be one of those who quietly disappear."

Well, happily, if England win in Australia, Edrich and Underwood will both be playing prominent parts. Underwood may always be happier on the more variable English wickets, yet I believe, because he is an intelligent man and has a very big heart, that he will still be a very good bowler overseas. He is improving all the time.

And this goes for Edrich too. He improves every day. He had

always been a very underrated batsman, in my opinion. If he stays in the game over the next three or four years it would not surprise me if he became the world's outstanding batsman.

The captain of a touring party is lucky if he can have good fast bowlers, but when I captained my first tour abroad in the West Indies in 1968 I had no Trueman, Statham or Tyson. Yet I considered myself very lucky in the selection of Snow, Brown and Jones. Jones has been forced to retire, but let us hope the others will be fit enough to lead the attack for England for another year or two ahead. They are big hearted cricketers who are better when they are up against it, but at the same time they are very different from each other.

John Snow has been born with a perfect physique and you could not find a better athlete. He is a glorious fielder with a lovely throw and is a genuinely fast bowler when he hits his rhythm.

David Brown might not be so gifted as the other two, but like Tony Lock, is a tremendous trier. It would not matter what time you asked him to bowl, which end, whatever the weather, he would summon up energy from somewhere and give you everything — and he can be a very nasty proposition to bat against, perhaps more so overseas than at home.

I shall always remember Jeff Jones batting in that last over at Georgetown, when victory in the series depended upon his surviving six balls. He survived. He was another who would give you everything and bowl all day if necessary. He was genuinely very fast and bowled an awkward bouncer. For several years his rather disappointing performances in England belied his true skills for I believe he was on the fringe of becoming a truly top class bowler. His injury has been both a personal tragedy and a great blow to English cricket.

I have the highest admiration for Geoffrey Boycott. Sometimes, perhaps, he has deserved reprobation but I really do feel he has been too much maligned. He is a very good games player, trying to do the best both for himself and his team. We are all made differently and, clearly, he has found genuine extrovert laughter irrelevant to the issue of getting runs, so, with single-mindedness he has not allowed it to intrude. As he tastes a little more success, as I am sure he will, I believe he will find that a bit more fun here and there, can be the necessary lubrication to oil the wheels of the nervous system. And this is a very important aspect of top class competitive sport. However, you will not find me casting a stone at Geoffrey Boycott, for I admire his great qualities.

As I said earlier, I am an optimist – and it takes quite a lot to be an optimist in cricket these days. The County balance sheets which appeared in the Spring were enough to shake anyone's confidence, but really it is not surprising. Personally, I was rather pleased that the warning red light has shone so dramatically. It has brought home to us all that there are very few major sports able to survive without being underwritten by sponsorship. We have resisted it for a long time. We have allowed it to come in gradually. Experience with the Gillette Cup and the Players' Sunday League should now have taught us that sponsorship can be acceptable without spoiling the game.

I feel very strongly that the County Championship should be maintained by the seventeen counties, or as many as would like to participate and that it should be financed from a central pool – the money provided by a sponsor, he getting his full return from dignified advertising. I think the central pool idea is essential so that each county is set up on a similar basis. All credit to Essex that they reduced their playing staff to thirteen and so made a profit. But I think they would be the first to admit they could have been in a lot of trouble. Had they lost a couple of players to Test Matches or through injury their members would have been watching them slip to bottom place and I do not think it would have been very fair to the rest of the side. I think of a wholehearted cricketer like Robin Hobbs, who might have had to watch two other players go to Test cricket or injury, and he would have had to try and bolster a team which simply was not good enough for the Championship. I would like to see the central pool finance a nucleus of sixteen fully fledged players in each county, thereby ensuring a proper wage to each one of the players. I would also like to see each county allocated some money from the central pool to take on, say, four youngsters, thus ensuring that there are apprentices being supported in each county. One of the sad things about our cutting down these last few years has been the fact that counties simply have not been able to take on sufficient youngsters. This is of particular importance, for it is quite impossible for cricket committees or coaches to pick out one young player and guarantee he is going to make the top grade. If you are able to take on three or four then you have the chance that one of them – the one who at first may look the least likely – might have the fighting temperament which drives him through. That fighting temperament could not possibly be in evidence in a few practice games. When the crunch comes, it comes hard and, had he not been taken on the group, he might never have had the chance.

I want a central pool to finance the umpires. The umpires' lot has improved enormously and with it the general standard has risen most noticeably. Mr. S. C. Griffith, the Secretary at Lord's, can be given a lot of the credit for this development, for very early in his secretaryship he saw the need to raise the standard of umpiring and this particular department has been his own baby. I still think there is room for improvement, and the central pool, backed by sponsorship, could bring them a little more money and better conditions.

Again, I look to see the central pool finance a head groundsman in each county, maybe two major grounds in each county. We have had some disastrous instances in recent years where a commercial firm has been able to lure away our best and most promising groundsmen and there was little that the county cricket club could do about it. Although our grounds are in better order, better fertilised, better mown, in better-looking order as each year goes by because of more modern methods, I am by no means convinced that the wickets are good enough; in fact, I think it is quite the opposite. I believe they are getting too much of modern methods and machinery, in looking after the wickets when I believe we want the old type of groundsman, the countryman who used the more time-consuming methods to produce the goods.

The central pool might be able to help with covering and sight screens, facilities which through shortage of money, we have had to forget about and muddle through. Where we would have been in Test Matches without Warwickshire's quite remarkable contribution providing a magnificent cover, I just don't know.

I can see all these improvements coming and the game progressing from strength to strength.

On the technical side I have a lot of hope for the change in the lbw law. It is so difficult to envisage the exact consequences of any change within the game and it will be a year or so before we can be certain of the effects. I am looking for a little more freedom for the batsman; part of the freedom, in fact, that we took away from him in 1935 when we changed the lbw law, and in doing so, gave so much to the bowler.

We may have to help further by lessening the seam on the cricket ball. When these extra stitches were allowed after the war it made a difference, and who would have thought it would have made all that difference? Already we have experimented with a cricket ball with less stitches and it looks as if there might be a reversion here. Further assistance will come with the continued improvement in the standard of wickets, I hope. People have just realised that good wickets do make for better cricket and that our wickets generally have deteriorated beyond what is reasonable. I am confident that we are going to see the batsman freed again because at last the cricket world sees this as a vital need and wants to see the change.

With regard to the general standard of cricket, I believe it is rising all the time. True, so much of it is not as entertaining as in years gone by but this can be accounted for by the fact that the balance between bat and ball is too equal. Once we can shift that balance to give the batsman the advantage, then we shall see more of the dominant batsmanship that we had become accustomed to in the '20s and '30s. There can be no argument, surely, that the fielding skills reach a higher standard with every year. There is no doubt in my mind that the modern cricketer is fitter than any cricketers have ever been — and younger on average. More thought is put into bowling than ever before and certain bowling skills are more developed I believe. The fielding pattern today is much more organised and prepared. Technically speaking, I think probably the batting has improved just as much but not in the way that the cricket world wants. We all ache for the batsman to break loose and collar the bowling more often.

Desperately I hope that there might be a shift towards more slow bowling in the '70s. Maybe reducing the stitching on the ball could help in this direction, but there will have to be other aids. Constantly the modern cricketer has found that on the wickets upon which he is asked to play, medium pace is both more economical and brings more reward than the genuine slow bowling – unless the slow bowling is of exceptional class.

Lastly, I hope that we can present our game aright. We must preserve the basic, old-fashioned tenets. Let us hope that the Test Match, England v Australia or England v West Indies will always remain a great attraction to watch, and for the aspiring cricketer the goal of his ambition. To provide players of Test Match standard we must keep sufficient of the first class County Championship game and I hope that sponsorship will make this possible. I have no fears for the John Player Sunday League nor the Gillette Cup for they are now established entertainment. I think this presents the ideal cricket balance.

As we move into the '70s I earnestly hope that the youngsters will continue to find the sort of magic which caused me to lose my heart to the game.

Index